The Dandie Dinmont Terrier

Its History and Characteristics

COMPILED FROM THE MOST AUTHENTIC SOURCES

By CHARLES COOK

Illustrated by Portraits of Authentic Specimens of the Pure Breed, Drawn and Etched by W. Hole, A.R.S.A.

EDINBURGH: DAVID DOUGLAS, CASTLE STREET

MDCCCLXXXV

Edinburgh University Press:
T. and A. CONSTABLE, Printers to Her Majesty.

TO THE MEMBERS OF

THE DANDIE DINMONT TERRIER CLUB

This Tribute

TO THE EXCELLENCE OF THEIR

CANINE FAVOURITES

IS RESPECTFULLY DEDICATED

PREFACE.

In publishing this small treatise it would almost seem that some apology is due, for there is an impression in many quarters that the history and characteristics of the Dandie Dinmont Terrier are subjects exhausted long ago. This may be true as regards a few of the leading breeders whose knowledge of the Pepper and Mustard race is doubtless extensive, but as regards those of the general public interested in the breed it is undoubtedly not so, for, notwithstanding the oceans of printer's ink which have been spent during the last twenty years anent this game little dog, there still exists much ignorance concerning the breed. Nay, worse than this: since the institution of Dog Shows throughout the length and breadth of this country a spurious type of Dandie has arisen, which, unless exposed, might in course of time have come to be considered by another generation 'who knew not Joseph' to be the 'Simon Pure.' The Dandie Dinmont Terrier Club has done much towards correcting the erroneous ideas held by many concerning the breed, but much remains to be done. The object of this little work is to help the Club, however slightly, in its praiseworthy endeavour to preserve the true race of Peppers and Mustards. My endeavour therefore has been to bring together, in a collected form, everything that has been said or written of the genuine Dandie Dinmont Terrier worth recording, so as to focus, if possible, its history and characteristics, and thus to enable any one 'taking up' the breed to start with some of the knowledge hitherto possessed only by a few breeders who have had the traditions of the race of Peppers and Mustards transmitted orally to them by an older generation.

The treatise therefore does not claim to have any literary pretensions, but only to be a matter-of-fact and faithful record of a very interesting and game breed of terriers as described by the best authorities on the subject.

Regarding the Illustrations, it may be explained

that to obtain reliable and satisfactory portraits of the Dandie Dinmonts of a former generation proved much more difficult than the Author anticipated, for, where authentic portraits have been obtained, it was often impossible to get faithful copies made, photography failing as a rule to convey a correct idea of the original. The Illustrations given, however, drawn and etched by Mr. W. B. Hole, A.R.S.A., can be relied on as being accurate. I have to thank Mr. Hole much for the careful study he has bestowed on the subjects of his etchings, which will, I think, be found to have considerable interest, and to be useful when contrasting old with modern authentic specimens of the pure breed, and also in illustrating the text.

The Map of the 'Dandie Dinmont' country may also prove interesting and instructive, as showing the original habitat of the breed.

In conclusion, the author has to record his most sincere thanks to that veteran breeder of the Dandie Dinmont, Mr. Francis Somner, late of West Morriston, now of Kelso, and to Mr. J. B. Richardson, Dumfries (also a well-known authority on Dandies), both of whom have given much useful information on the subject of this work. Thanks are also due to the representatives of the late Mr. Eaglesfield Bradshaw Smith, for kindly placing the invaluable Blackwoodhouse records—extending from 1841 to 1882—at the Author's disposal, and from which much interesting matter has been derived.

Indeed, some may think possibly that Mr. E. B. Smith and the Blackwoodhouse kennel are too often referred to; but this has simply been matter of necessity, for had it not been for Mr. Smith all authentic connection with the breeders and dogs of a former generation would have been lost. This is not meant to infer that no pure-bred Dandies were to be found except in the Blackwoodhouse kennel, but that none existed outside of it which could to any degree approach Mr. Smith's terriers for authenticity or length of pedigree.

C. C.

EDINBURGH, *March* 1885.

CONTENTS.

APPENDIX.

ILLUSTRATIONS.

THE

DANDIE DINMONT TERRIER.

CHAPTER I.

The supposed origin of the Border breed of Terrier now known as the 'Dandie Dinmont'—The breed when first known confined to the Northumbrian Borders—The Border 'Muggers'—'Piper' Allan and his dogs—*Guy Mannering*—James Davidson of Hindlee *alias* 'Dandie Dinmont of Charlieshope'—The sources from which Davidson obtained his Terriers—Public attention called to the breed—The 'Davidson Writing'—Does the pure breed still exist?—The Blackwoodhouse Records.

THE exact origin of the now historic race of 'Peppers and Mustards,' or 'Dandie Dinmont' Terriers, is practically unknown, notwithstanding all the investigations and lively discussions which for many years past (particularly from 1867 to 1880) have been maintained, almost without intermission, in the leading sporting journals by those interested in the breed; and it may now be safely affirmed that the *actual origin* of the race will never be definitely ascertained.

Nor indeed should this fact be matter of surprise, for unless it is to be affirmed that the earliest known specimens of the breed were a pair which Noah had with him in the Ark, the race of Peppers and Mustards must, like all other members of the great canine family, have been either the result of 'chance,' or the product of 'selection' *à la* Darwin carried on for very many years, the law that 'like begets 'like' doubtless ultimately occasioning the permanent fixture of the type.

Many theories have however been from time to time propounded as to the origin of the race of terriers now called Dandie Dinmonts, the most generally accepted one being that of an original cross betwixt the old Scotch terrier (a dog now extinct) and the rough Welsh harrier or Otter-hound, with a dash of pure bull-dog blood thrown in to give courage and tenacity of purpose,—followed by careful selection so as to preserve in the 'terrier' certain characteristics of the 'hound.' The hound cross, it is maintained, is clearly shown in the formation of the teeth and ears, and in the general 'houndy' carriage and appearance of the 'stern' of the Dandie. It is pointed out, however, with considerable force, by those who disbelieve in this theory, that none of these ingredients would account for the mixed coat and silky covering on the head of the pure-bred Dandie, neither old Scotch terrier, bull-dog, nor hound having at any rate the least symptom of a silky 'top-knot.' Further, if this otter-hound and Scotch-terrier cross theory were correct, it would be only probable that terriers showing similar characteristics to the Dandie would be found elsewhere than in the Borders of Scotland and England. This not being so, however, one is rather led to suppose that the materials out of which the Pepper and Mustard race were evolved were peculiar, or at any rate confined, to the Border district. A more plausible theory (although one quite as speculative as the other) is that the Gypsies (who originally came to this country from the Continent) had, on their effecting, in comparatively early times, a lodgment in the Borders, been accompanied by foreign terriers of the Dachshund type, and that these were crossed by them with the terrier of the district, viz., a dog much of the old-fashioned 'Yorkshire' terrier type,—not the toy variety of the present day, but an active, hardy, bustling terrier, rather leggy and small-boned perhaps, with profuse silvery-blue coat, dark eyes, and sharp terrier face,—the cross ultimately resulting in the Pepper and Mustard race. Those who uphold the purity of the Dandie as a distinct breed, on the other hand, deny all *cross* theories, and maintain that the race is simply the product of long years of careful breeding, or selection (the native rough terrier being alone employed), the requirements of the Border Country ultimately producing a terrier adapted for its special work; and to this latter theory I am personally disposed to incline.

All such theories, however, being purely speculative, no real good can be served by their discussion. It is more to the purpose to trace the breed back to the earliest date at which it is known to have been considered a distinct race of terriers, and to ascertain, if possible, with some degree of certainty, what its appearance and characteristics then were, and whether these are exhibited in the dogs of the present day.

So far as I have been able to ascertain from conversations I have had with old breeders, and from the few stray references to the early history of the breed which are to be found in books, the race of terriers under consideration (for in its early days the breed had no specific name) does not seem to have been indigenous specially to Scotland, but to have been distinctly a *Border* breed of terrier,—the race being cherished equally on both sides of the Cheviots. Mr. Francis Somner, one of the few remaining original breeders of the 'Dandie Dinmont,' I remember, in a conversation I had with him, was very clear on this point. 'The race of Peppers and Mustards,' he said, 'was not originally a Scotch terrier, but was a 'Border breed. Where they originally came from, 'or how they were originally bred, no one can now 'say, but when first known to history they were con-'fined very much to the Coquet Water district in 'Northumberland, and were in the possession of the 'Border "tinkers" and "muggers,"—chiefly among 'the Allans, Andersons, Anguses, Faas, and others, 'who cherished their breed of terriers much as the 'Arabs are said to cherish their horses, their little 'four-footed friends sharing "bed and board, bite '"and sup," with their masters. These terriers 'were apparently, one might say, placed in that wild 'country, and designed by Nature for the extermina-'tion of foxes, otters, polecats, and such vermin 'as were to be found in the district.'

One family in particular in that district was long famous for having the purest and gamest strain of terriers, viz., the Allans of Holystone, near Rothbury. Chief of this family was the famous Willie Allan, or 'Piper' Allan[1] (the name he was better known by), who was born at Bellingham in the year 1704, and who was nominally a 'tinker,' but whose principal occupations seem to have been

[1] See Mr. Robert White's letter in Dr. John Brown's *Horæ Subsecivæ*.

playing on the bagpipes and hunting the otter. The Piper resided principally at Holystone or 'Holestene' on the Coquet Water, near Rothbury, Northumberland. He was a skilful fly-fisher and keen sportsman. 'Among his other pursuits,' writes Mr. Robert White to Dr. John Brown,[1] 'he 'excelled especially in the hunting of otters, and 'kept eight or ten dogs for that particular sport.' History records that the Piper had three special favourites among his terriers, viz., 'Charley,' 'Hitchem' (sometimes erroneously called 'Peachem'), and 'Phœbe.'

Many stories are told of the performances of the Piper's dogs. 'Lord Ravensworth,' says the same authority, 'once employed Willie to kill the otters 'that infested his pond at Eslington Hall, which 'he soon accomplished; and on going away, the 'steward, Mr. Bell, offered, in his Lordship's name, 'to buy "Charley" at the Piper's own price. Will 'turned round very haughtily, and exclaimed, "By '"the *wuns*, his hale estate canna buy 'Charley'!"' 'Hitchem,' or 'Peachem,' 'was Will's chief favourite, 'and such confidence had he in the animal, that 'when hunting he would at times observe, "When '"my 'Peachem' ('Hitchem') gi'es mouth"' (that is, marks the otter in his holt), '"I durst always

[1] See *Horæ Subsecivæ*, quoted *ante*.

'"sell the otter's skin."'[1] On another occasion it is said the Duke of Northumberland offered a liferent lease of a small farm to the Piper in exchange for 'Hitchem,' 'but after deliberating 'for a day, Allan said, "Na, na, ma Lord, keep yir '"ferum; what wud a piper do wi' a ferum?"'[1]

'He died on 18th February 1779, aged 75 years, 'and was buried in Rothbury churchyard.'[1]

The Piper was succeeded by his son James, who was born at Hepple, Coquetdale, March 1734. He also was a great player on the pipes, and a well-known 'character' at all the Border race-meetings, fairs, etc. He died at Durham, November 13th, 1810, aged 76. He in turn was survived by a son, who by the way sold to Mr. Francis Somner at Yetholm a terrier dog named 'Old Pepper,' the lineal descendant of his grandfather's famous dog 'Hitchem.' 'Old Pepper' was one of the great-grandsires of Mr. Somner's famous dog 'Shem.'

The race of terriers thus cherished by the Allans and others on the Borders are the earliest known ancestors of the breed now known as the 'Dandie 'Dinmont' terrier. It was, in a limited way, from the itinerant habits of its possessors, to be found here and there in the Border counties in the hands

[1] See *Horæ Subsecivæ*, quoted *ante*.

of the neighbouring county gentlemen, farmers, and sportsmen, who now and again had obtained specimens of the breed as a favour, or perhaps more generally *for* a favour, from members of the Allan, Anderson, or other nomad families.

The fame of the breed, however, did not extend beyond the immediate vicinity of the Northumbrian border until after 1814, in which year Sir Walter Scott, 'the Wizard of the North,' first published his well-known Border tale, *Guy Mannering*.

It seems that Sir Walter, while sojourning in the Borders, when Sheriff of Selkirkshire, had heard of the renown of various of the 'Store-farmers' and shepherds, and their terriers, as hunters of the fox and otter, in the hills and dales of the then wild Border country, and with his usual facility, when writing *Guy Mannering*, he wove into his romance the charming character of 'Dandie Din-'mont,' the burly tenant of 'Charlieshope,' with his inimitable race of terriers, 'Auld Pepper and Auld 'Mustard, and Young Pepper and Young Mustard, 'and Little Pepper and Little Mustard.'

The original of 'Dandie Dinmont' was the late Mr. James Davidson, tenant of the hill-farm of Hindlee, in the parish of Southdean, and county of Roxburgh, who 'was a great fox-hunter, and his 'breed of terriers—the pepper-and-mustard class—

'were the best over all the country,"[1]—and whose odd manner of calling all his terriers by the generic names 'Pepper and Mustard,' according to their colour, and without further individual distinction, had seemingly 'tickled' Sir Walter Scott's sense of humour.

Public attention having thus been drawn to the race of terriers kept by Mr. Davidson for hunting the fox, badger, and otter, the breed became very popular and much sought after, and as 'Stonehenge' stated in an article on the Dandie Dinmont terrier in the *Field* of 5th May 1877, 'Davidson and his 'neighbour, Mr. Somner, of West Morriston, near 'Kelso, bred great numbers of Dandies, to meet the 'demand created by Scott, and the breed gradually 'spread.'

In these early days the majority of people who possessed specimens of the Pepper and Mustard race did not pause to inquire where or how James Davidson became possessed of his race of terriers, but were satisfied to rest content with the knowledge that their dogs were of 'Dandie Dinmont's' breed; and it was not until these latter days of dog-shows and disputes, doubts and discussion, that inquiries came to be made as to whether the race of Peppers and Mustards were the actual

[1] See *Horæ Subsecivæ*, quoted *ante*.

creation of James Davidson, or a previously existing Border breed which he merely had a fancy for, and kept for the purposes of hunting the fox and otter.

The vast majority of the public, I dare say, were under the impression that the 'Dandie Dinmont' terrier *was* created by Mr. Davidson, and the result of various crossings of different breeds, but those who knew the Borders were well aware that the race of Peppers and Mustards was in the hands of others besides Mr. Davidson, and had for long been known to exist as a distinct race previous to his getting possession of the breed ; that in point of fact Mr. Davidson's terriers were of the same race and blood as those long cherished by the Allans, Andersons, and others in the Northumbrian Borders.

What is now a matter of great importance, however, was not thought of at all, when the information could have been readily obtained, and so the question of where Mr. Davidson procured his terriers presents some little difficulty at this time in answering precisely.

According to Mr. Francis Somner, West Morriston, before mentioned, the foundation of James Davidson's strain of terriers came from 'Holestene' or Holystone, on Coquet Water, and were of the Allans' breed. This view is also held by Mr. Paul Scott, Jedburgh, another veteran breeder of the

Dandie Dinmont terrier, who informed me that Ned Dunn, Whitelee (Carterbar), also procured his terriers from the same source.

'Stonehenge,' in the first edition of his book *The Dog in Health and Disease*, published in 1859 (the article on the Dandie being, I believe, practically the joint production of Mr. James Aitken, Maryfield House, Edinburgh, a veteran breeder of the Dandie, and Dr. Sidey of Edinburgh), also states that Davidson was supposed to have got his dogs from the head of Coquet Water,[1] and Dr. John Brown ('Rab'), in relating the history of 'Our Dogs,'[2] makes special mention of '"Crab," 'the *Mugger's* dog, grave, with deep-set, melancholy 'eyes, as of a nobleman (say the Master of Ravens- 'wood) in disguise, large-visaged, shaggy, indomi- 'table, *come of the pure Piper Allan's breed*,' and adds that from a famous dog of the Piper's 'de- 'scended Davidson (the original Dandie Dinmont) 'of Hyndlee's breed, and "Crab" could count his 'kin up to him.'

That the Allans, and others in the Borders, had preserved the race of terriers for which 'the 'Piper' had been in his day so famous, down to the time of James Davidson, there can be no doubt,

[1] See *The Dog in Health and Disease*, by Stonehenge, 1859.
[2] See *Horæ Subsecivæ*, mentioned *ante*.

for Mr. Francis Somner, as before mentioned, actually purchased himself at Yetholm, from Piper Willie Allan's *grandson* (whose name was Allan, and who was also, like his grandfather, a basketmaker), the dog named 'Pepper,' which was the lineal descendant of the old Piper's famous dog 'Hitchem.'

The following account of the origin of the Dandie appeared in the *Field* of 7th December 1878, and, while amusing, has every probability of truth, as regards the fact, at any rate, that James Davidson got some of the produce of the terriers referred to in the letter, although, of course, it is absurd to allege that the whole race of Peppers and Mustards sprang from this union. The letter of Mr. Davison, besides, is of some importance as confirming the statement that the Border 'muggers'' terriers were the real source from which sprang the 'Dandie Dinmont.' It runs thus:—

'Sir, I, as rather more than a sexagenarian and a 'Border man, and one who in almost his childhood 'took up with Dandies, can, I think, throw some 'light on the origin of the Dandies possessed by 'Mr. Davidson. The Border "muggers" were 'great breeders of terriers—the Andersons on the 'English side, and the Faas and Camells on the 'Scotch side. In their perambulations they gene'rally met once or twice a year at Long Horsley,

'Rochester (the ancient Bremenium of the Romans), 'Alwinton, or some other Border village. If they 'could not get a badger, they got a foumart, wild-'cat, or hedgehog, at which to try their dogs. The 'trials generally ended in a general dog-fight, which 'led to a battle-royal amongst the tribes represented. 'This afterwards led to a big drink and exchange of 'dogs. Jock Anderson, the head of the tribe, had a 'red bitch, who, for badger-drawing, cat, foumart, 'or hedgehog killing, beat all the dogs coming over 'the Border. Geordy Faa, of Yetholm, had a wire-'haired dog terrier, the terror of not only all other 'terriers in the district, but good at badger, fox, or 'foumart. They met at Alwinton, where Willy and 'Adam Bell (noted terrier-breeders) had brought a 'badger they had got hold of at Weaford, near the 'Cheviots. Both the red bitch and other black 'terrier drew the badger every time they were put 'in. "Jock Anderson," says Geordy, "the dogs '"should be mated; let us have a grand drink, the '"man first doon to lose his dog." "Done," says 'Jock. They sent for the whisky, which never 'paid the King's duty, to Nevison's, at the little 'house, having agreed to pay 2s. a quart for it. 'Down they sat on the green, fair drinking; in 'eighteen hours Jock tumbled off the cart-shafts, and 'Geordy started off with the dogs. They were 'mated, and produced the first Pepper and Mus-'tards, which were presented by Geordy to Mr. 'Davidson (Dandie Dinmont of *Guy Mannering*); 'strange to say, the produce were equally the colour 'of pepper and mustard. The last pair I saw of 'what I consider perfect Dandies were Robert 'Donkin's, at Ingram, near Alnwick, just before I 'left the North in 1838. I have been at shows, 'but could never identify any Dandies shown as at 'all like the original breed belonging to the Telfords 'of Blind Burn, the Elliots of Cottonshope, the 'Donkins of Ingram, and other Border farmers. I 'am not a doggy man, but like to see all old breeds 'kept distinct. 'J. DAVISON.[1]

'ANDOVER, *Dec.* 2.'

There seems then to be no reason to doubt that the terriers belonging to the Allans, Andersons, Faas, and others in the last century were of exactly the same race and blood as the terriers which belonged to James Davidson and others in the Borders in the beginning of the present century, and which, after the production of *Guy Mannering*, were first called 'Peppers and Mustards' (according to Sir Walter Scott's nomenclature), and ultimately 'Dandie Dinmonts.'

In these latter days, however, 'chapter and verse'

[1] See the *Field* of 7th December 1878.

must be given along with any statement of fact; hence, in the discussion of the 'Dandie Dinmont' in the *Field*, when a letter appeared in that journal's issue of 13th November 1869 announcing the discovery of a document alleged to be in the actual handwriting of the veritable James Davidson himself, containing the names of the Adam and Eve of the 'Dandie Dinmont' race, great was the rejoicing among a certain class of breeders. Men like Mr. Francis Somner, who knew of the breed having been in the hands of the Allans, and others, long before, and also possessed by Mr. Thomas Stevenson, Jedburgh, and others, coevally with Mr. Davidson, smiled at the notion of Davidson being thus made the originator or creator of the race of Peppers and Mustards. But such men do not trouble themselves much with discussions in the papers, and so the writing was allowed to pass for a time, and was pretty generally accepted by the Dandie Dinmont 'fancy' as authentically accounting for the origin of the Dandie Dinmont terrier.

The 'discoverer' of this alleged writing was the Reverend J. C. Macdona of Cheadle Rectory, Cheshire, a gentleman well known as a judge of dogs, and his name, I have no doubt whatever, made the document in question be much more readily accepted than it might otherwise have been.

Mr. Macdona's letter was in these terms :[1]—

'I have, however, in my researches into the history 'of this breed in this neighbourhood' [the letter is dated from Melrose], 'near to its early home, this 'day been fortunate enough to meet with a docu-'ment in Mr. James Davidson's own handwriting, 'to which his initial signature is attached. The 'perusal of this paper has convinced me as to the 'real origin of the Dandie Dinmont terrier. The 'document bears all the marks of genuineness. The 'writing is yellow with years. The paper is the 'old-fashioned hand-made letter-paper, none of that 'cream-laid note, straw or satin, so much used 'now-a-days. *It was sent by Mr. Davidson to the 'late Hon. George H. Baillie of Mellerstain*,[2] and 'runs thus :—

'" 1800.

'" Tuggin, from A. Armstrong, reddish and wiry.
'" Tarr, reddish and wire-haired; a bitch.
'" Pepper, shaggy and light, Dr. Brown of Bonjedward.
'" The race of Dandies are bred from the two last.

'" J. D."'

Now the observation which at once occurs to any one reading this document as above quoted is

[1] See the *Field* of 13th Nov. 1869.

[2] The italics are mine.

this :—The document bears the date 1800, and the word 'Dandies' occurs in it. But *Guy Mannering* was not published until 1814, and the generic name 'Dandies' as applied to the Pepper and Mustard race of terriers was unquestionably unknown previous to the publication of Sir Walter Scott's novel. The question then comes to be,—Is the date in the document the date on which it was written, or is it meant to show the date on which Mr. Davidson first got his terriers? This matter is one which, so far as I am aware, has not been hitherto noticed or discussed in any of the sporting papers or elsewhere, although it must have occurred to many who read Mr. Macdona's letter, and no public explanation of the apparent discrepancy has yet been made.

So far as I am aware, no one ever attempted publicly to discredit the discovery, except in 1873, when the Dandie was again under discussion in the *Field*. In that year, however, a very important statement regarding this supposed writing of Davidson's was made in a letter to that paper by 'A 'Border Gypsy,' who wrote :[1]—'I may assume a 'right to have my say out on this subject, *being the 'owner of the paper referred to by Mr. Macdona*[2] in 'his letter of Jan. 31' [Mr. Macdona had again referred to the Davidson writing], 'who dis-

[1] See the *Field* of 8th March 1873. [2] The italics are mine.

'covered it just "where Allan Gregor faund the '"tings." As this paper has on several occasions 'been quoted as an authority, it may gratify your 'readers to hear how it came into my possession.

'*It was obtained from Mr. Davidson by a Mr. 'Dempster*,[1] in those days a great Dandie fancier, 'given by him to Mr. Scott of Newstead, and I took 'it as a present from him, as I knew best how to 'keep it.'

The observation which will now occur to the reader will be: 'Stop a moment; there is surely 'another discrepancy regarding the document here, 'for did not Mr. Macdona, in his letter in 1869, state 'that the writing was sent by "Mr. Davidson to '"the Hon. George H. Baillie of Mellerstain," while 'now the *owner* of the paper says that "it was '"obtained from Mr. Davidson by a Mr. Dempster," 'given by him to Mr. Scott, and then taken pos-'session of by "A Border Gypsy"?'

But further, 'A Border Gypsy' boldly asserts that Mr. Macdona discovered the writing 'where 'Allan Gregor faund the tings;' or, in other words, that there was no 'discovery,' so to speak, at all! The next question which arises, therefore, is: From whom did Mr. Macdona obtain his information in 1869 regarding this paper? If from its then owner,

[1] The italics are mine.

Mr. James Scott, Newstead, then from whom did 'A Border Gypsy' get the other account of the writing? There is a discrepancy here which undoubtedly requires explanation.

By the courtesy, however, of its present possessor, I had an opportunity lately given to me of personally examining this somewhat mysterious document, and the result of my examination has been to perplex me still more regarding it.

The original writing runs thus:—

'1890
red. & wirie
'Tuggin from A. Armstrong
redush & wirie skind
'Tarr ^ D— Bitch D——
Shaggie & ligh ward
'Pepper, ^ Dr. Brown Bonjed
'the race of Dandies are
'bred from the two last
'J. D.'

First, I would ask the reader to observe the date, which is not 1800, as given by Mr. Macdona, but *1890* (!), or only twenty-one years *post*-dated from the year of its discovery; not to mention that the year 1890 is at the present time only a possibility in futurity. I am informed, however, that the document was written about the year 1818, and that in the circumstances under which it was produced (after dinner), a 'slip of the pen' was a most probable occurrence, and an oversight of the mistake as to the date quite excusable at the time.

However, be this as it may, the mistake seriously injures the worth of the document, even if undoubtedly genuine otherwise.

The text of the original paper, it will also be noticed, exhibits several material differences from the hitherto accepted version. For instance, from it it would rather seem as if 'Tarr' as well as 'Tuggin' had been received from 'A. Armstrong,' the D's with the 'dash' after them, occurring after the word 'Tarr,' evidently in the original document standing for 'Ditto, Ditto.' But hitherto it has been accepted as a fact that 'Tarr' and 'Pepper' both came from 'Dr. Brown, Bonjedward'!

I have been at considerable pains to try and, if possible, unravel the tangle of discrepancies with which this document is encompassed, but without success. 'A. Armstrong,' the alleged donor of 'Tuggin,' is believed to have been Andrew Armstrong, a shepherd on the farm of Wooplaw (James Davidson's birthplace); but of him and 'Tuggin' we do not need to inquire further, as 'Tuggin' is not alleged to have had anything to do with the origin of the 'Dandie Dinmont' race. Bonjedward is a village in Roxburghshire, in the neighbourhood of Jedburgh, but of 'Dr. Brown, Bonjedward,' I have been unable to learn anything, or to get any information as to his terriers; nor can I discover any one, even among such veteran fanciers as Mr. Francis Somner, Kelso, Mr. James Aitken, Edinburgh, Paul Scott, Jedburgh, Hugh Purves, Leaderfoot, etc. etc., who can give me any information as to Dr. Brown or his terriers.

Besides the apparent discrepancies I have just alluded to, there is a final difficulty which I have to state regarding this unfortunate paper. It is this, and is perhaps the most important of all. The handwriting in the original document has puzzled me very much, being quite dissimilar from the ordinary writing of James Davidson of Hindlee, if I may judge from specimens of his signature written in the year 1817, and exhibited to me by his grand-nephew, Mr. Richard Davidson, Swinnie, near Jedburgh. Comparing these signatures (which were appended to a legal document) with the writing in the paper under discussion, there is the most unmistakable difference. The writing in the latter is bold, business-like, and free, while Mr. Davidson's signatures (which were all identically the same in character and formation) are written in a cramped and unbusiness-like hand, evidencing the unaccustomed penman's anxiety to form correctly every letter,—in short, just such an unpractised hand as one would naturally have expected 'Dandie Dinmont' to have written. Now I think it is fair to presume that Mr. Davidson could write his own name in as bold and free a hand at least as any other of his writing, yet if we are to accept this paper anent the origin of Dandies as authentic, we must believe that at the same period at which it was written, James Davidson, while writing it in this bold free hand, could only with some difficulty sign his own name! Had the document in question been written in the cramped hand, and the signatures to the legal paper been written in a bold free hand, the circumstances under which the former was written might have been referred to by way of explanation of the discrepancy. The case, however, is *vice versa*, and therefore hard to understand.

The initials 'J. D.' are written in a somewhat different hand from the writing in the body of the paper, but yet they too are totally unlike these initial letters as appearing in Mr. Davidson's signatures before alluded to.

Thus, before this document can be admitted to be authentic, the following points require to be cleared up:—

1. The discrepancies between the statements made respectively by Mr. Macdona and 'A Border

'Gypsy' in the *Field* regarding its origin and history.

2. Its true date, and the interpretation of the date it actually bears.

3. An explanation of the occurrence in the document of the word 'Dandies,' bearing in mind that *Guy Mannering* was first published in the year 1814, and that Mr. Davidson died in the commencement of the year 1820, and that between these dates his race of terriers was generically called 'Peppers 'and Mustards.'

4. The identification of 'Dr. Brown, Bonjedward,' and his breed of terriers.

5. Proof that the writing in the original document is the handwriting of James Davidson of Hindlee, or at least that the initials 'J. D.' were appended by him to the document.

As in the case of the account of the origin of the Dandie Dinmont given by Mr. Davison already referred to, the theory originated by this alleged writing of James Davidson of Hindlee, viz., that the whole race of 'Peppers and Mustards,' or 'Dandie Dinmonts,' sprang from one pair of terriers—'Tarr' and 'Pepper'—is manifestly absurd, for, as was well pointed out by 'Corsincon' in an article on the breed in the *Country* of 1st June 1878, 'Pepper and Tarr must have had relations,' brothers and sisters and cousins, and uncles and aunts, who were as much entitled, so far as breeding and appearance were concerned, to be called 'Dandie Dinmonts,' and to be bred from as such, as those bred by Mr. Davidson. Besides, as I have shown, the Pepper and Mustard race were in the hands of the Allans and others long before as well as at the same period at which they were in James Davidson's possession.

Further, Mr. Robert White states that 'the 'mother of the far-famed *Peppers* and *Mustards* was 'a *dark*-coloured, rough-haired bitch of the name 'of "Tar,"'[1]—and not *reddish*-coloured, as stated in the writing.

With all these considerations before me, and in the absence of any satisfactory explanation on the points before alluded to, I think this alleged writing of James Davidson is unworthy of serious consideration, — because even if it were properly authenticated it would not account at all for the *origin* of 'Dr. Brown's' terriers, far less for the whole race of Peppers and Mustards. I here therefore dismiss this document, with the explanation that it has only been referred to by me at such length from its having been so often quoted by other writers on the Dandie Dinmont as accounting for

[1] See *Horæ Subsecivæ*, quoted *ante*.

the origin of that breed of terrier, whereas, as I have shown, the Pepper and Mustard race were in existence long before the period the paper can possibly refer to.

In the *Field* of 30th January 1869 there had, previously to the publication of the alleged 'David-'son Writing,' appeared an article by 'A Border 'Sportsman' which gave an interesting enough 'Historical Account of the origin, progress, and 'decline of the Pepper and Mustard Terrier.' From the allusion in this article to the mysterious 'Dr. 'Brown, Bonjedward,' I think we may safely assume that 'A Border Sportsman' was Mr. James Scott, Newstead (or at least some one drawing his information from him), for his account of how James Davidson first became possessed of his famous race of terriers is evidently based on the 'Davidson Writing,' which at that time was 'undiscovered,' as far as the public were concerned, although presumably in the hands of Mr. Scott. I here quote from 'A Border Sports-'man's' article, however, only for the purpose of showing that Mr. James Scott, whose knowledge of the Dandie was undoubtedly extensive, practically admitted in that article that the race of Peppers and Mustards existed at the period when Mr. Davidson first got his terriers, *as a distinct breed in*

Coquetdale, and that consequently he did not *create* that race of terrier, but merely perpetuated an existing breed. It follows therefore that terriers descended from Davidson's breed would not necessarily differ from the terriers of other breeders, except in so far as his peculiar principles of selection in breeding might differ from those of other breeders, thus gradually tending to establish a more or less distinct type of his own.

When I come to discuss, however, the characteristics of the Dandie Dinmont terrier, I shall show that all the old breeders adhered to the same original type, and bred on the old lines, besides taking care to preserve the old blood.

'A Border Sportsman'[1] then states that 'in the 'year 1800 Andrew Armstrong presented the 'young sportsman, James Davidson, with a fox-'hound, and a terrier, named Tuggin, and shortly 'after he received from a Dr. Brown, Bonjedward, 'the famous bitch "Tar" (mentioned by Dr. John 'Brown in *Horæ Subsecivæ*), and a dog named 'Pepper. Tuggin was of the breed common in 'that wild country—a dog that could make his way 'anywhere; a compact, tallish terrier, red ochre 'in colour, with wiry hair.

'It is not, however, of him that I have to write,

[1] See the *Field* of 30th January 1869.

'but of the other two terriers, Tar and Pepper. 'These were both very small, and very short in the 'leg, with long bodies, large and long heads, ears large 'and pendent, like a hound's or beagle's, but a little 'more pointed in the lower end. Tar was reddish 'ochre in colour, with rough wiry hair; Pepper was 'quite shaggy in coat, and of a creamy ochre colour.

'About this time young Mr. Davidson got the 'farm of Hindlee, on the Rule Water, on the 'estate of Lord Douglas; and soon after this a Mr. 'Stephenson, the tenant in Plenderleigh, *procured 'for him another of those small terriers.* It was *no 'relation to those he already had, being from Roth-'bury, on the Coquet Water,* WHERE THAT PECULIAR 'SMALL BREED WAS TO BE FOUND *in the greatest per-'fection, and bred by the Allans,*[1] Andersons, and 'Anguses. This Rothbury specimen was very dark 'in colour and very rough in coat. The descendants 'of these three form the first of the Pepper-and-'Mustard or Dandie Dinmont race of terriers. . . .

'The true breed was quickly spread among Mr. 'Davidson's friends and brother sportsmen,—the 'Davidsons of Swinnie, the Telfers of Blindburn, 'Lilicoes of Jedwater, Bells of Hundalee Mill, and 'Ned Dunn of Whitelea. But next to Dandie 'Dinmont himself for keeping up and distributing

[1] The italics are mine.

'the pure race at an early period of its history 'were the Hon. G. H. Baillie of Jerviswoode and 'Mellerstain, and Mr. Home of Carrolside. . . .'

Whether Davidson's terriers were procured by him from this particular person or that, is, however, not of much moment, provided it is clearly understood that they were no new breed, but belonged to a race long before his time known and valued as a pure breed of terriers on the Borders.

Since James Davidson's time the breed of 'Dandie Dinmont' terrier has, carefully and continuously down to the present time, been preserved pure and untainted by a few admirers of the breed, and to whose kennels all the pure-bred 'Dandies' of to-day trace back.

That pure-bred Dandies exist now-a-days has been, however, denied by some, but there is not a shadow of a doubt that there are still many of the true breed in existence.

In 1869 this question was put to James Scott of Newstead :—Did he consider or believe that there was a pure-bred 'Dandie' in existence? His emphatic answer was,[1] 'Most decidedly I do. 'I believe that Mr. Robson, Mr. Dodd, etc., have 'them in the vicinity of the Redswire, as also 'others; that Mr. Aitken, Mr. Bradshaw Smith, 'Mr. Milne all have them, and many others; I

[1] See the *Field* of 4th December 1869.

'even believe that Mr. Mosse and Mr. Macdona 'are in possession of pure Dandies. Let us re-'member what numbers of the very purest went to 'England in presents; the number of pure, mingled 'among the mongrels, sent to London alone by the 'dog-dealers; to these I am sorry to add the great 'numbers sent to London, etc., Edinburgh, Glasgow, 'etc., by the dog-lifters, *alias* stealers. If a judicious 'care had been taken, the purest breeds should 'have been in abundance in England, Scotland, 'and even in Ireland.'

Whatever may have happened to the great numbers of the pure breed originally sent here and there throughout this country, there is no doubt whatever but that, so far as concerned the kennels of Mr. Francis Somner, West Morriston, James Kerss, Bowhill, old John Stoddart, Selkirk, Mr. M'Dougal, Cessford, Mr. Frain, Trows, Mr. James Scott, Newstead, Mr. Milne of Faldonside, Mr. E. Bradshaw Smith of Blackwoodhouse, and perhaps one or two others, the breed of Dandies was maintained in all its purity, and through them has been handed down to the present time untainted.

To prove this statement promised at one time to be somewhat difficult, as, while the fact is notorious that 'all the most celebrated breeders strongly 'maintain that they have kept to the lineal de-'scendants of the original "Pepper" and "Mustard" 'immortalised by Scott,'[1] these breeders, for obvious reasons, have not cared during their lives to make the pedigrees of their dogs public property, and at their deaths seldom leave their stud memoranda in such a state as to be followed or understood by others. The papers left by the late Mr. E. Bradshaw Smith of Blackwoodhouse, however, are fortunately 'the exception which proves the rule,' and in them are to be found ample evidence of the correctness of the statement.

In the Appendix will be found certain pedigrees of Dandies taken from the Blackwoodhouse Records, which are sufficient to show, so far as this can be done in such a work as this, that at the present time there are terriers in existence whose pedigrees trace back in direct line, 'on both sides of the house,' to the Hindlee Peppers and Mustards. The pedigrees in the Blackwoodhouse Records have been drawn on to prove the continuity of the pure race, not only on account of the fact that this kennel existed continuously in the possession of the late Mr. E. B. Smith for nearly half a century, but also from the stud records left by Mr. Smith being so complete and unimpeachable, his notes having been made from day to day throughout this long period.

[1] See 'Stonehenge's' article on the Dandie Dinmont terrier in the *Field* of 5th May 1877.

In giving these pedigrees I would close the more strictly historical part of my subject, explaining that it must be distinctly understood that I have purposely refrained from attempting more than to trace the history of the race of Dandie Dinmonts from the earliest known period down to comparatively recent times, and to show that the pure race was in the hands at any rate of one breeder whose kennel was only dispersed in 1882. I have, however, thought it right to add to the Appendix the pedigrees of two modern prize-winning Dandies (whose portraits are also given), to show that dogs having authentic pedigrees can, and do, win prizes at our dog-shows,—which proves the gratifying fact that the old and true type is once more being recognised and appreciated. 'Tweedmouth' and 'Border Queen' have been selected for this purpose, not from any wish to extol them in any way, but simply from the fact that they are both well known to the public, and are good specimens of their race.

More might have been perhaps done in the way of quoting authentic pedigrees, but it is enough if the continuity of the pure breed of Dandie Dinmont terriers has been shown to be unbroken, in even the case of one kennel (Mr. Smith's), from the time of James Davidson of Hindlee to the present time.

CHAPTER II.

The early breeders of the Dandie Dinmont Terrier.

In the preceding chapter I have endeavoured to trace the history of the Pepper and Mustard race from the earliest known times down to the present, showing that long before the advent of 'Dandie Dinmont of Charlieshope' the breed was established and well known on the Borders, although it was not until after the publication of *Guy Mannering* that it received the generic name 'Pepper and Mustard'—afterwards changed to 'Dandie Dinmont'—became famous, and so better known and more widely distributed than it had been formerly.

Whenever the 'rage' for these terriers, however, had thus set in, they were bred to an extent before unknown on the Scottish Borders, by many persons besides Mr. Davidson, namely, neighbouring country gentlemen, sportsmen, farmers, gamekeepers, etc. Accordingly it seems proper that I should here give a list of the more prominent early breeders of the pure race of Pepper and Mustard terrier, the names being as far as possible chronologically arranged.

First and foremost, of course, comes Mr. James Davidson, Hindlee, *alias* 'Dandie Dinmont of Charlieshope;' while after him come Messrs. David and Arthur Kyle, Braidlee; Mr. Taylor, Whitelee; Ned Dunn, Whitelee (Carterbar); the Duke of Buccleuch; the Duke of Northumberland; the Duke of Roxburghe, the Hon. George Hamilton Baillie of Mellerstain and Jerviswoode; Sir Walter Scott of Abbotsford, Bart.; Lord Polwarth; the Marquis of Tweeddale; Mr. Thomas Stevenson, Jedburgh; Mr. Francis Somner, West Morriston, near Earlston; Hugh Purves, Leaderfoot; Mr. Wm. Reid, Jedburgh; R. Pringle, Esq. of The Haining; Mrs. Douglas, Old Melrose; John Stoddart, Selkirk; Mr. D. M'Dougal, Cessford; Mr. W. Frain, Trows; Home of Carolside; the Davidsons —Swinnie, Wooplaw, and Arks (relatives of 'Dandie Dinmont'); Telfers, Blindburn; Lilicoes, Jedwater; Bells, Hundalee Mill; Henry Dodds, Jedburgh; Armstrongs, near the Redswire; Walter Ronaldson, Darnick; T. Simpson, Esq., Blainslie; James Kerss, gamekeeper at Bowhill; Wm. Scott, Teviotbank; Scott, Wauchope; Wm. Johnstone, Lilliesleaf; John Lauder, Bemerside; Sir George H. S. Douglas of Springwood Park, Bart.; W. Broadwith, Longnewton; Mr. James Scott, Newstead; Mr. James Aitken, Maryfield

House near Edinburgh; Nicol Milne, Esq. of Faldonside; John Stewart Lyon, Esq. of Kirkmichael; Makdougal Brisbane, Esq. of Makerston; Dr. William Brown, Melrose; Dr. John Brown ('Rab'), Edinburgh; Mr. Lang, Selkirk; Dr. Grant, Hawick; and last, but not least, E. Bradshaw Smith, Esq. of Blackwoodhouse, near Ecclefechan, Dumfriesshire.

Besides these there were of course many others of lesser note, on both sides of the Border, who owned and bred the pure 'Pepper and Mustard.' Of those named, however, I may perhaps briefly notice more particularly the more prominent.

JAMES DAVIDSON, HINDLEE.

I have already in the preceding chapter mentioned the sources from which Mr. Davidson derived his race of terriers, but it may be interesting that there should here be given some account of himself, and how he came to be made the prototype of 'Dandie Dinmont of Charlieshope,' by Sir Walter Scott, in *Guy Mannering*.

Sir Walter tells us[1] that the character of 'Dandie 'Dinmont' was drawn from no individual in particular. 'A dozen at least of stout Liddesdale 'yeomen with whom he has been acquainted, and 'whose hospitality he has shared in his rambles

[1] See note to chapter xxiv. of *Guy Mannering*. Cadell and Co., Edinburgh, 1829.

'through that wild country' (the Border hills), 'at a 'time when it was totally inaccessible save in the 'manner described in the text, might lay claim to 'be the prototype of the rough but faithful, hos-'pitable and generous farmer. But one circum-'stance occasioned the name to be fixed upon a 'most respectable individual of this class, now no 'more. Mr. James Davidson of Hindlee, a tenant 'of Lord Douglas, besides the points of blunt 'honesty, personal strength, and hardihood, de-'signed to be expressed in the character of Dandie 'Dinmont, had the humour of naming a celebrated 'race of terriers which he possessed by the generic 'names of Mustard and Pepper (according as their 'colour was yellow or greyish black), without any 'other individual distinction, except as according 'to the nomenclature in the text. Mr. Davidson 'resided at Hindlee, a wild farm on the very edge 'of the Teviotdale mountains' (parish of South-dean, and county of Roxburgh), 'and bordering 'close on Liddesdale, where the rivers and brooks 'divide as they take their course to the eastern 'and western seas. His passion for the chase, in 'all its forms, but especially for fox-hunting, as 'followed in the fashion described in the twenty-'fourth chapter' (of *Guy Mannering*), 'in con-'ducting which he was skilful beyond most men in 'the South Highlands, was the distinguishing point 'in his character.' James Davidson above referred to was born at the farm of Wooplaw, on the north side of the Redswire, towards the end of last century. When still a young man he became tenant of the farm of Hindlee above mentioned, where he remained until within a year or two of his death, which occurred in 1820.

Sir Walter Scott further tells us that 'when the 'tale' (*Guy Mannering*) 'on which these comments 'are written became rather popular, the name of 'Dandie Dinmont was generally given to him, 'which Mr. Davidson received with great good-'humour, only saying, while he distinguished the 'author by the name applied to him in the country, 'where his own is so common,—"that the Sheriff '"had not written about him mair than about other '"folk, but only aboot his dogs." An English lady 'of high rank and fashion, being desirous to possess 'a brace of the celebrated Mustard and Pepper 'terriers, expressed her wishes in a letter, which 'was literally addressed to Dandie Dinmont, under 'which very general direction it reached Mr. 'Davidson, who was justly proud of the application, 'and failed not to comply with a request which did 'him and his favourite attendants so much honour.'[1]

[1] See note to *Guy Mannering*, quoted *ante*.

In a letter[1] addressed from Abbotsford in April 1816, Sir Walter describes his first introduction to 'Dandie Dinmont' in the following amusing manner: —'I have been at the Spring Circuit, which made 'me late in receiving your letter, and there I was 'introduced to a man whom I never saw in my life 'before, namely, the proprietor of all the Pepper 'and Mustard family, in other words, the genuine 'Dandie Dinmont. Dandie is himself modest, and 'says "he b'lives it's only the dougs that is in the '"buik, and no himsel'." As the surveyor of taxes 'was going his ominous rounds past Hyndlee, 'which is the abode of Dandie, his whole pack 'rushed out upon the man of execution, and Dandie 'followed them (conscious that their number greatly 'exceeded his return), exclaiming, "The tae hauf '"o' them is but whalps, man!" In truth, I knew 'nothing of the man, except his odd humour of 'having only two names for twenty dogs. But 'there are lines of general resemblance among all 'these hillmen, which there is no missing; and 'Jamie Davidson of Hyndlee certainly looks Dandie 'Dinmont remarkably well. He is much flattered 'with the compliment, and goes uniformly by the 'name among his comrades, but has never read 'the book. Ailie used to read it to him, but it

[1] See Lockhart's *Life of Scott*, vol. iv. p. 3.

'set him to sleep. All this you will think funny 'enough.'

In hunting, we are told by Mr. Dixon in *Field and Fern*,[1] Mr. Davidson 'did not care for a pack 'of dogs, and with a shepherd or two to help him, 'two hounds, and the terrier bitches Tug and Tar, 'he was about a match for any Liddesdale fox. Be 'it foulmart, cat, or even a collie dog, he had a turn 'at it. He always went over to Abbotsford, and 'met Hogg, Laidlaw, Captain Clutterbuck, etc., 'at the annual coursing meeting, when Sir Walter, 'with Maida at his feet, watched from a hill the 'doings of what the latter evidently considered an 'inferior race. It was a merry night at Selkirk, 'and the Club mull went round with Sir Walter's 'own inscription, "May the Foresters never want a '"friend at a pinch." Tom Potts, than whom there 'was no hunting shepherd of "stronger bone and '"firmer pith," always said that Dandie "never '"hunted with the same glee after he brought the '"wife hame." Still, he kept Nimrod, a cross 'between a greyhound and a fox-hound, to the 'last; and he rose from a sick-chamber, mounted '"Dimple," and, with Nimrod at his heels, obeyed 'the summons to see a bagman from Deadwater

[1] *Field and Fern, or Scottish Flocks and Herds* (*South*), by H. H. Dixon, 1865. Rogerson and Tuxford, *Mark Lane Express* Office, 246 Strand, London.

'Fell turned out for him at Burnmouth. This was 'in the year '19.'

A year or two before the expiry of his lease of Hindlee, Mr. Davidson, who had fallen into bad health, retired from farming and Hindlee. He died on 2d January 1820, survived by a widow, two sons, and a daughter, the last of whom, I understand, alone now (1885) survives.

'Dandie Dinmont died,' a friend writes to Sir Walter Scott,[1] 'on the first Sabbath of the year '(1820); an apoplectic stroke deprived him in an 'instant of all sensation, but happily his brother 'was at his bedside, for he had detained him 'from the meeting-house that day to be near him, 'although he felt himself not much worse than 'usual. So you have got the last little Mustard 'that the hand of Dandie Dinmont bestowed.

'His ruling passion was strong even on the eve 'of death. Mr. Baillie's fox-hounds had started a 'fox opposite to his window a few weeks ago, and 'as soon as he heard the sound of the dogs his eyes 'glistened; he insisted on getting out of bed, and 'with much difficulty got to the window, and there 'enjoyed the fun, as he called it. When I came 'down to ask for him, he said "he had seen '"Reynard, but had not seen his death. If it had

[1] See note to *Guy Mannering*. Cadell and Co., Edinburgh, 1829.

'"been the will of Providence," he added, "I would '"have liked to have been after him; but I am glad '"that I got to the window, and am thankful for '"what I saw, for it has done me a great deal of '"good."'

It is not surprising that the Pepper and Mustard race have acquired a fame which, I venture to think, no other breed of dogs can equal, for the immortal genius of Sir Walter Scott has not only pictured to us in a way peculiarly his own the charming character of the honest, sturdy, kindly 'Dandie Dinmont,' but has invested his race of terriers with a double interest; and we should love the breed even for its old master's sake, apart altogether from its own intrinsic worth, as one of the best and gamest terriers in existence.

THE KYLES, BRAIDLEE.

After James Davidson, Hindlee, perhaps David and Arthur Kyle, Braidlee, had greater names as fox-hunters among the Cheviot Hills than any one else. Mr. Dixon, in his interesting work, *Field and Fern*,[1] thus alludes to the brothers:—'David 'Kyle of Broad Lee, beloved of Lord John Scott, 'could not be called, like Scott of Singlee, "a

[1] *Field and Fern, or Scottish Flocks and Herds*, by H. H. Dixon.

'"singular grand divine among sheep," but he was 'quite a shepherd's friend in his line, and though 'he might be led at first in the hunt, no shepherd 'could live with him till the close of day. He would 'not keep a shepherd who could not hunt, and his 'brother Arthur was nearly as keen. Kyle once 'ran against Routledge, laird of *The Flatt*, at 'Christenbury Creggs, near Newcastleton. He 'never met a better man, according to his own con-'fession, but Routledge thought himself as good, '"bar louping the hags." Davie had no great 'hound language, but he loved to have all the dogs 'around him when he had a dram, and then he was 'highly colloquial both with them and his friends. 'He lived at the head of Hermitage Water, and as 'a stock farmer he had one peculiarity—his tups 'must all be horned. Liddesdale and Teviothead 'were the cream of his country, and from New Year's 'Day till April he would be there with a dozen or 'fifteen shepherds at sunrise, each provided with a 'pocket-pistol and a lump of bread and cheese.

'Old Kyle was a good wrestler and fighter for 'his inches. In early days he was entered to hare, 'but he changed to fox after thirty, and killed nearly '800 brace in his fifty years. Cauldcleuch and 'North Tyne furnished some of his best foxes, 'which were all of the greyhound breed, and took a 'world of catching. He always knew them again, 'or said he did, and spoke of them confidentially as 'old acquaintances. The drag was generally hit off 'from certain syke-heads, and when the foxes did 'go to ground they were always "spaded" and 'never smoked. Bolting them for "an afternoon '"fox" was not the custom of the hunt. His terriers 'were of the Dandie Dinmont breed, and latterly, 'as the neighbours said, he looked like a terrier 'himself.' David Kyle died in 1861.

THE DUKE OF BUCCLEUCH.

The late Walter Francis, Duke of Buccleuch and Queensberry, K.G., was in his earlier days a keen fancier of the Dandie Dinmont terrier. His Grace's brother, Lord John Scott, also took a great interest in the breed, and the kennels at Bowhill contained therefore for a long period some of the choicest specimens of the Pepper and Mustard race. Duke Henry, third Duke of Buccleuch, and grandfather of the late Duke, had been in his day also famous for his terriers, which were of the old Border breed from which have sprung, as I believe, the Dandie Dinmont. An etching of the head of one of these terriers, from a picture painted in 1770, is given at p. 66. The chief sources from which the Bowhill kennel was supplied in the time of the late Duke were:—James Davidson, Hindlee, Sir Walter Scott, and old John Stoddart of Selkirk. James Kerss,[1] of Dandie Dinmont fame, succeeded Fletcher as gamekeeper at Bowhill at Whitsunday 1834, and for many years afterwards he maintained the breed with great care at Bowhill. For some years previous to Kerss' death, which happened comparatively lately (1880), the Bowhill terriers had almost disappeared, but traces of the kennel are still to be found in the pedigrees of many of the best dogs of to-day, where the names of the Duke, Lord John Scott, and James Kerss the Bowhill keeper, are to be found as owners of Dandie Dinmonts.

SIR WALTER SCOTT

got his terriers presented to him by 'Dandie 'Dinmont' himself. Of Sir Walter's terriers, however, little is now known, but in the papers left by the late Mr. E. Bradshaw Smith there occurs this memorandum, of date 1st June 1843, which shows that he kept up the breed: 'Lord Polwarth, 'Mertoun, had a brace of terriers given to him 'by Sir Walter Scott, who got a brace from Mr.

[1] James Kerss, a son of 'Rob of the Troughs,' was born at Kelso on 12th July 1805. He died at Shielshaugh on 8th March 1880, aged seventy-five years, having been head-keeper at Bowhill for forty-six years. He was buried at Kirkhope, and over his grave stands a cross with this inscription: 'This Cross is placed to his memory by Walter Francis, Duke of Buccleuch, 'out of regard for one who did his duty in singleness of heart, fearing God.'

'Davidson of Hindlea—*alias* Dandie Dinmont of 'Charlieshope. Sir W. Scott's are dead. Lord 'Polwarth has now only one, a dog,—very old, 'colour grey and tan, or blue and tan,—same as Sir 'Walter Scott's,—very handsome.' This terrier was much used as a stud dog, and the name of 'The Mertoun Dandie' appears in almost every pure-bred Dandie of the present day. Mr. E. B. Smith's memorandum is interesting, because it confirms the purity of Lord Polwarth's dog's breeding, and states that Mr. Smith considered him 'very 'handsome.' The latter remark is one to bear in mind when considering the appearance of a pure-bred Dandie.

Mr. Lyon of Kirkmichael, Dumfriesshire, also got a pair of Dandies from Sir Walter Scott, and there exists at Kirkmichael an oil painting, done in 1848, of certain members of the family, into which two terriers of this breed are introduced.

Mr. Thomas Stevenson, Jedburgh,

was one of 'Dandie Dinmont's' most intimate acquaintances and companions in hunting the fox amongst the Cheviot Hills. He kept up a splendid kennel of Peppers and Mustards, and in his day was considered a first-rate judge of the breed. Among others, the Marquis of Tweeddale, and

Mr. Francis Somner, West Morriston, got some of their terriers from Mr. Stevenson.

Old John Stoddart

was a blacksmith at Selkirk, who at one time was said to have the purest strain of the Dandie Dinmont breed in the Borders. Between 1820 and 1830 John Stoddart had his famous pair of Dandies, Dandie I. and Schan. The former he got from Mr. ———, Darnick, before that gentleman went abroad, and the latter came from Hindlee direct. In the Blackwoodhouse records Dandie I. is described as 'a very handsome dog—colour, light 'grey and tan; short legs, very broad behind. The 'most game dog of his day.' Of Schan, Mr. Smith says, 'She was a little dark-grey bitch from Hindlee '(under-jaw projected). She was very game.' 'Both dog and bitch are now dead' (Mr. Smith writes in 1843), 'but J. S. bred several pups from them:—

'1. His own dog Dandie (II.). Colour, light 'grey and tan. Age, nine or ten years.

'2. Mr. Tod of Drygrange got one darker grey, 'very good, not out of same litter as Dan' (Dandie II. above), 'but a previous one two years 'before. His name was Charlie; now dead.

'3. Lady Ravensworth got a pup.

'4. The Duke of Buccleuch got a bitch, like its mother, under-hung. It killed rats when eight weeks old. Now dead.' (This bitch was Bowhill "Schan.")

'5. A pup was sent to ——— in Edinburgh.

'6 and 7. M'Culloch, Hot Baths, Leith, got a 'dog and bitch which he sold to Mr. Lyon, Kirk- 'michael, Dumfriesshire.

'8. Mrs. Douglas, Old Melrose, got a bitch 'named Wasp. Now dead.

'Colour of these pups was either dark or light 'grey, or blue, and all proved very game.' There were besides these many others which were sent to various other persons.

The famous dog 'Charlie,' belonging to Thomas Tod, Esq. of Drygrange, No. 2 above mentioned, was only 13 lb. weight, but was very game, and on one occasion when the Duke of Buccleuch's hounds had run a fox to earth near Drygrange, 'Charlie' was sent for, and when put into the drain at once tackled the fox, his Grace ultimately 'tailing' Charlie, and pulling out him and the fox in presence of the whole field.

John Stoddart was always very particular as to the purity of his terriers, taking the greatest care to use nothing but the 'bluest' blood in breeding.

As an instance of this I may quote the words of

an old Selkirk breeder of the Dandie Dinmont, Mr. Thomas Welsh, who says, 'I think one of my 'first excursions out of the old Border burgh was 'with Jocky (Stoddart), to help him to carry '"Musk," a bitch that I think "Old Dandy" was 'bred from, up to Bowhill. So careful was the old 'man, that the bitch was put into a bag, and carried 'on his back. I spoke of this to Mr. Kerss, his 'Grace's head-keeper, a short time ago (1879), 'when he told me he minded of the thing quite 'well. When he told Jocky he might have led 'her up on a string, "Ay," says Jocky, "she has '"less chance o' fa'ing in love wi' onything on the '"road when she's on our back."' A good proof this that the old breeders were most careful to preserve the pure blood of the Pepper and Mustard race.

R. Pringle, Esq. of The Haining,

had his best dogs from John Stoddart, Selkirk. The pure breed was maintained at The Haining until 1843, when, after Mr. Pringle's death, the kennel was dispersed. Mrs. Douglas, Mr. Pringle's sister, who resided at Old Melrose, also was a keen Dandie fancier, and had many dogs of great excellence in her possession.

MR. FRANCIS SOMNER, WEST MORRISTON, among the original breeders of the Dandie Dinmont terrier since James Davidson's time, takes a very prominent place. Mr. Somner's famous kennel was founded somewhere about the year 1820, when he procured a small pepper-and-salt coloured bitch named 'Nettle,' which was bred at Hindlee.

Mr. Somner tells of his getting Nettle thus :—

'Mr. Thomas Stevenson, Jedburgh, before men- 'tioned, had come over with a few hands to help 'my father, who farmed largely near Haddington, 'with the harvest. I was going into the harvest- 'field one day, when suddenly something rushed at 'my legs, and seized me by the trousers. I looked 'down, and saw a curious-looking little dog, more 'like an otter than anything else, being long in the 'back, with very short legs. I had never seen any- 'thing like it before, and I called out to Mr. 'Stevenson to come and see the creature. When he 'came he said, "Oh! that's a Dandie Dinmont's '"terrier. She came over with one of James David- '"son's men from Hindlee. It is one of the breed '"referred to in *Guy Mannering*." I looked again 'at the little creature, and then noticed that it had 'been sitting on a coat (her master's) at the edge of 'the field, and I was so taken with its appearance 'that I said to Mr. Stevenson that I would like to 'get it. He told me the breed had lately come into 'great request, and that I would have to pay a long 'price for her. I then saw the owner and bought '"Nettle." This occurred somewhere about 1820, 'I think, but might be a few years earlier.'

For the next thirty years Mr. Somner kept up a splendid kennel of Dandies, his dogs approaching very nearly perfection in shape, colour, and gameness, and being in great request among admirers of the breed. Of the many Dandies bred by Mr. Somner, however, the best was probably his famous dog 'Shem' (whelped 1839), which was a direct descendant of 'Nettle.' Of 'Shem' further notice is made in the Appendix. When Mr. Somner gave up his country life, about 1842, and went to live in Kelso, he partly broke up his kennel, the greater number of his dogs going to the kennels of Mr. E. Bradshaw Smith, 'Old Shem' being among them. He however kept a few of his famous strain about him, selling in June 1844 a brace of Dandies to Count Robert de Portalis, who bought them for the then King of France, Louis Philippe. In the year 1852 Mr. Somner finally dispersed his kennel.

Mr. Somner was very particular in entering his dogs properly before using them as stud dogs. As an example of the high nature of the trials his dogs had to pass before he considered them good enough to use at the stud, I may cite the case of 'Pepper,' referred to at p. 7. Shortly after he had got 'Pepper,' from Allan, the basket-maker at Yetholm, Mr. Somner tried him four days in succession at badger. On the fourth day 'Pepper' was so much swollen about the head and throat that Mr. Somner hesitated much trying the dog again, both on account of the pain it would give 'Pepper,' and also half doubting if the dog would in the circumstances face so fierce a foe as a badger. However, a badger was boxed, and 'Pepper' brought out, when, the moment he was loosed, he went into the box (which was nine feet long, and ingeniously contrived, so that if a dog got into difficulties with his antagonist he could be rescued), and fought the badger with the greatest determination, notwithstanding that he was stiff and sore from the wounds inflicted on the three previous days, and ultimately 'drew the brock.' In fact, all had to stand the test with fox, badger, otter, etc., before they were thought worthy of being bred from. This he considered essential for the proper preservation of the wonderful gameness for which the race of Peppers and Mustards had always been so famous.

DR. WILLIAM BROWN, MELROSE,

and his brother, Dr. John Brown ('Rab'), were also keen Dandie fanciers. In *Horæ Subsecivæ*, in a chapter on 'Our Dogs,' Dr. John Brown gives an interesting notice of the breed. 'Crab,' 'John 'Pym,' and his son 'Puck,' were perhaps the most famous of their dogs.

JAMES SCOTT, NEWSTEAD,

was another keen fancier. First and last, he had as great an experience of the pure breed as any one, and in the pedigrees of the best dogs of the present day the names of Mr. Scott's old favourites are to be found. Like Mr. Thomas Stevenson, Jedburgh, Mr. Scott knew James Davidson, Hindlee, personally, and as a lad hunted the fox with him among the Cheviot Hills. In the discussion on the Dandie in the *Field*, in 1869, Mr. Scott took an active part, and contributed much valuable information regarding the breed. He died at Newstead on 18th June 1874.

MR. NICOL MILNE OF FALDONSIDE

got his first Dandie Dinmont terrier from his brother-in-law, Mr. Wilson of Otterburn, who is said to have possessed a 'Mustard' which had belonged to James Davidson of Hindlee, and which was very game.

Mr. Milne also procured from the widow of Ned Dunn, the Whitelee gamekeeper, a yellow bitch named 'Jenny,' whose sire was yellow and mother black and tan. Of 'Jenny' Mr. E. Bradshaw Smith in the Blackwoodhouse Records says, under the date 1st June 1843, 'She is *very* good.'

'Jenny' was a famous bitch in her day, and was much bred from. Her progeny, like herself, were very good. As will be noticed later, Mr. E. Bradshaw Smith got several of them, viz., 'Tot' by 'Drygrange Charlie,' the sire of Somner's 'Shem;' and 'Jock' and 'Dandie (B)' by Dr. Brown's 'John 'Pym,' a son of Somner's 'Shem.'

Although Mr. Milne carefully kept up during his life a first-rate kennel of Dandies, it is to be regretted that he left no written records of his dogs.

Mr. John Stewart Lyon of Kirkmichael, Dumfriesshire,

as before mentioned, procured a brace of Dandie Dinmonts from Sir Walter Scott somewhere about 1820. Some amateur and rather unfinished sketches of Mr. Lyon's dogs still hang in Kirkmichael

House. These, however, it is to be regretted, are not of much value as delineating correctly the originals from which they were made, viz., 'Old 'Pincher, an old soldier;' 'Juno, favourite of Col[l] 'Ross, 1830;' and Spicy 'by Sir Walter Scott's 'original Pepper, 1825.' There is also a picture of some members of the Lyon family, painted by Gibson of Edinburgh about 1848, in which are introduced two terriers, viz., a Pepper named 'Spicy,' and a Mustard named 'Witchy.' As in the case of the sketches above referred to, the portraits of 'Spicy' and 'Witchy' are not very satisfactory. Mr. Lyon also bought from M'Culloch of the Hot Baths, Leith, a dog and bitch bred by old John Stoddart, Selkirk, by his Dandie I. out of Schan, from Hindlee. These terriers, crossed with the ones obtained from Sir Walter, founded the Kirkmichael strain. For many years Mr. Lyon kept up the pure breed, but after his death the Kirkmichael kennel gradually fell away, and now is a thing of the past.

MR. JAMES AITKEN, MARYFIELD HOUSE, EDINBURGH,

procured his first Dandies about the year 1840. In 1846 he obtained the bitch 'Meadow,' mentioned in the first edition of 'Stonehenge' (1859).

She was bred in December 1844 at Birseslees, Longnewton, Roxburghshire, being by Sir George H. S. Douglas of Springwood Park's 'Pepper,' out of his 'Schann.' 'Schann' was by the Duke of Buccleuch's 'Old Pepper' out of his Grace's 'Schann,' by old John Stoddart of Selkirk's Dandie I. out of 'Schann,' from Hindlee. 'Pepper' (Meadow's sire) was bred by Mr. Lang, Selkirk. It should be here mentioned that some confusion has arisen between Mr. Aitken's 'Meadow' and the famous 'May-day' belonging to D. M'Dougall, Cessford, and afterwards to Mr. E. B. Smith, Blackwoodhouse. This has probably arisen from the phonetic resemblance of the names 'Meadow' and 'May-day' when pronounced in the Scottish dialect.[1] About the same period (1846) Mr. Aitken obtained a young dog from Dr. William Brown of Melrose, named 'Shem.' He was by Dr. Brown's famous dog 'John Pym' (a son of Mr. Somner's 'Shem') out of a bitch of Mr. N. Milne of Faldonside. The progeny of this pair Mr. Aitken crossed with dogs of the Telfers, Blindburn, and other good strains, and at the present time he still possesses some of their descendants.

[1] The exception taken by Dr. Grant, Hawick, in *Field and Fern*, to Meadow's pedigree, as stated by 'Stonehenge' in his book on the Dog, evidently arose from the confusion between 'Meadow' and 'May-day' here alluded to.

Dr. Grant, Hawick,

was a sportsman in every sense of the word. Notwithstanding a large country practice, he found time to hunt the otter in the Teviot and other streams in the neighbourhood of Hawick with a small but carefully selected pack of otter-hounds and Dandies. Mr. H. H. Dixon in his work *Field and Fern*,[1] before alluded to, gives the following interesting account of Dr. Grant and his terriers :—

'To pass through Hawick without having an 'introduction to Dr. Grant and his Dandie Dinmonts 'was not to be thought of. We first met him in the 'outskirts, journeying professionally towards Teviot-'dale, with three of them in his dog-cart. Grey-'hounds, terriers, otters, and a good practice form 'his quadruple tie to the district, and he has almost 'ceased to think of his native Highlands. His 'house is a faithful reflex of himself. There is an 'infant badger stuffed on the staircase, and an otter 'of 25 lb. on the landing. . . . The Doctor's best 'affections have always been, not so much with the 'clan Grant, as with his Dandie Dinmonts, and his 'back-yard is quite a Charlieshope. Nettle and 'Pepper, from Paul Scott of Jedburgh, were the first

[1] *Field and Fern, or Scottish Herds and Flocks* (*South*), quoted *ante*, p. 40.

'arrivals; and Sir George Douglas's keeper gave 'him Shamrock, who had recently devoted himself to 'worrying collies. "Shammy" is of the Birseslees 'branch of the Dandie Dinmont family, referred to 'by "Stonehenge" *On the Dog*. He was bred by 'Mr. James Scott of Newstead, from Vixen by '*brown* Pepper, or Pepper, or "Pepper the Second." 'In short, the Doctor believes in no other blood 'than that which is derived from James Davidson of 'Hindley and almost primæval Pepper and Mustard 'renown. He had bought many things in Dandie 'shape before he cast in his lot with this breed, but 'his trials were too high for them. They were 'entered with rats, and mounted the scale to cats, as 'age and performance might warrant. Too many of 'the puppies stopped there, or did not get any 'further than a muzzled fox; and then, if age gave 'them solid confidence, they took their B.A. degree 'with the badger. This species of culture tends 'upwards to the otter, in which Tom and Teddy '(the sons of Shamrock and Nettle) have become 'quite Regius Professors. Teddy gains in pluck 'what he loses in style. He goes quietly up to the '"fish-slicer," and gets almost bitten to death on the 'head without a murmur, while he surely does the 'deed; but Tom dashes in with all the *élan* of a 'Zouave, and has it by the neck before it can get 'home with its "clinches." A retreat for purely '"strategic purposes" is a thing they wot not of.

. . . . . .

'Any one who dares to say that the Dandie is 'cross-bred must gird up his loins then and there 'for a vigorous course of polemics. Not only has 'the Doctor looked into the whole thing in a most 'learned note, but he can quote several lines from 'the Greek poet Oppianus, who flourished in the 'second century, to prove that the "crook-limbed '"and black-eyed" breed were natives of Britain at 'the time of the Roman invasion.'

Mr. E. Bradshaw Smith of Blackwoodhouse

was a native of Dumfriesshire, but, having property in Roxburghshire, went to reside there about the year 1840, and when there first became acquainted with, and an ardent admirer of, the Dandie Dinmont terrier. Mr. Smith may, I think, be fairly looked upon as the saviour of the pure breed of Dandie Dinmont terrier from extinction. Indeed, as a breeder of, and authority on, the Dandie Dinmont, he stands out pre-eminent from the time of James Davidson to the present day. Starting his kennel in 1841, Mr. Smith founded his strain of Dandie Dinmonts by the purchase of terriers of only the most undeniable blood, including dogs from the kennels of Mr. F. Somner, Hugh Purves, Leaderfoot; D. M'Dougall, Cessford; Frain, Trows; John Stoddart, Selkirk; Mr. Milne of Faldonside; J. Kerss the Bowhill gamekeeper; Mr. Pringle of The Haining, and others. The breed was maintained at Blackwoodhouse with the greatest care down to the date of Mr. Smith's death (1882), the variety of strains in his kennels enabling him to cross backwards and forwards throughout the greater part of this long period practically without going outside his own kennels for fresh blood. From time to time, however, to avoid the evil effects of too much 'in-breeding,' Mr. Smith added to his stud occasionally specimens of the pure race, making excursions for the purpose throughout the Borders to places where he knew he could obtain such,—his habit of making notes on the spot of the really good dogs in the various districts he visited and of their owners enabling him to insure the purity of the new blood. Writing on 27th February 1876, Mr. E. B. Smith says, 'Since 1854 'the only additions I have made to my kennel, save 'those I bred myself, are those I had from Mr. 'J. B. Richardson; Gyp (by Dr. Grant's "Teddy" 'out of Dr. Riddell's "Mary I.") from Mr. Pool; 'two pups from the Rev. S. T. Mosse, Jock by Dirk 'out of Captain Lyon's bitch, and Brock by Dirk 'out of Mr. Macdona's Meg, bred by Mr. Milne. 'In 1854 I purchased from Mr. Milne the last of 'the progeny of his famous old Jenny,' viz., 'Dandie (B)' referred to in Appendix III. Those from Mr. Richardson, I may add, were 'Jock' and 'Jenny' by Mr. Smith's 'Pepper' (sire of Dirk, Appendix III.) out of Mr. Richardson's 'Myrtle' in 1868, and at subsequent periods several other grown dogs and puppies, nearly all sired by Mr. Smith's own dogs, and out of well-bred bitches belonging to Mr. Richardson. Among these may be mentioned the handsome Mustard dogs 'Otter' and 'Badger,' both by Mr. Smith's 'Marmot' out of Mr. Richardson's 'Topsy,' whelped 3d April 1876.

The Blackwoodhouse terriers, as will be seen from the Appendices, were connected in direct line with the original Peppers and Mustards of Charlieshope. Mr. Smith kept careful stud notes of the breeding of all his terriers, together with the pedigrees of the various dogs purchased by him at different times, and a perusal of these notes would convince the most sceptical that in Mr. Smith's strain we possess lineal descendants of the famous Hindlee terriers.

Among the many famous Dandies acquired by

Mr. Smith I may specially mention 'Dandie II., bought from old John Stoddart of Selkirk, whelped about the year 1833, which died in December 1848 at the ripe age of fifteen years; a bitch, the last survivor of the terriers of Ned Dunn, the Whitelee gamekeeper (the contemporary and companion of James Davidson, Hindlee); 'Tot' by 'Drygrange 'Charlie' out of Nicol Milne's famous yellow bitch 'Jenny;' also 'Jock' and 'Dandie (B)' by Dr. Brown's 'John Pym,' a son of Somner's 'Shem' out of N. Milne's 'Jenny;' 'May-day,' a Pepper bitch whelped in 1836 or 1837, from Mr. D. M'Dougall, Cessford ('May-day's' brother was sold for a large sum to a French gentleman, who presented him to Louis Philippe); 'Ruth,' 'Whin,' and 'Shem' (the latter whelped in 1839, and whose pedigree is given in the Appendix), from Mr. F. Somner. Mr. Smith had, on one occasion, the honour of presenting in person one of his famous terriers to Her Majesty the Queen, at Windsor, who was graciously pleased to accept it.

The quality of the Blackwoodhouse terriers was always in the old days fully tested at badger and other 'large game.' 'So determined were they,' writes a correspondent, 'that many a badger was 'killed outright by some of the stronger dogs 'before they could be taken off, while some of the 'smaller ones of about 12 lb. weight would cling 'to their game with as much tenacity of purpose, 'although they had not the strength to punish so 'severely. When a very severe test was required, 'the dog was run at two badgers in the same box, 'and had to submit to the punishment of one while 'he held the other.'

In the autumn of 1880 a dastardly outrage was perpetrated at the Blackwoodhouse kennel, two dogs and three bitches being poisoned, but the miscreants were never brought to justice, notwithstanding the offer of a substantial reward for any information.

Mr. Smith died somewhat suddenly at Geneva on the 19th March 1882 (where, many years previously, he had buried 'Old Shem'), when on his way home from Switzerland, where he latterly wintered, and his kennel, which then consisted of seven dogs and six bitches, was shortly afterwards dispersed, with the exception of one Mustard dog, 'Birkie,' which was retained by Miss Smith as a house-dog.

CHAPTER III.

What constitutes a 'Dandie Dinmont terrier'?—'The Dandie controversies—The 'Dandie Dinmont Terrier Club'—The 'Club' standard of excellence.

TURNING now from the history of the Dandie Dinmont terrier and its early breeders, I come to the question,—'What constitutes a Dandie 'Dinmont terrier?'

In the beginning of 1869 this question was first raised publicly in a long and fierce discussion which took place in the *Field*, consequent on the curious judging of the Dandie class at Birmingham Show in December 1868, by Messrs. C. Collins and Matthias Smith, and although there was a great deal of nonsense as to the breed written, much useful information was then given by various writers. Foremost amongst the disputants was the Rev. S. Tenison Mosse, who, I must say, in spite of his detractors, did more for maintaining the true breed than any other writer, by inducing such men as Mr. Francis Somner, Kelso, Mr. James Scott, Newstead, Mr. James Aitken, Edinburgh, and

Mr. George Telfer, Blindburn—men who really knew what they were writing about,—to come forward and state their views as to the Dandie Dinmont in the *Field*, for the benefit of the public. The result of the discussion was to thrash out the subject and to get pretty well at the truth, although still every now and then the 'fire,' which was thought to have been put out, bursts out afresh in one or other of the sporting journals. This arises, I think, from the fact that the ranks of Dandie Dinmont 'fanciers' are from time to time being recruited by persons taking up the breed, who have previously been in total ignorance of its history and characteristics, neither of which are to be 'learned 'in a day.' These discussions will, however, be more fully noticed later on.

In answering the question of 'What is a Dandie?' I propose to adopt the plan indicated in the opening chapter, namely, having first traced the race of Peppers and Mustards back to the earliest period at which it was known as a distinct breed, to endeavour to ascertain what its appearance and characteristics then were, and thereafter to inquire whether that appearance and these characteristics are to be found in any of the modern representatives of the race.

I have explained that the Dandie Dinmont terrier

was originally a Northumbrian breed (although undoubtedly since the beginning of this century it has chiefly been bred on the Scotch side of the Border), and first heard of as a distinct race of terriers in the hands of Piper Allan the elder, the head of the Allan tribe, say about the year 1720. Is there any contemporary evidence extant as to the appearance of the Piper's terriers? The only reference to terriers which I have been able to find in natural-history books published about that period is in Bewick's well-known *History of Quadrupeds*.[1] This work was first published at Newcastle-upon-Tyne in the year 1790, and its information is valuable, not only from the date, but from the fact of its being the work of a Northumbrian, and published in Northumberland. Bewick, it is natural to suppose, would be most familiar with the breeds of terrier prevalent at the time in Northumberland, and in writing the article on the terrier would give a description of them.

'The terrier,' he says, 'has a most acute smell, 'is generally attendant on every pack of hounds, and 'is very expert in forcing foxes or other game out of 'their coverts. It is the determined enemy of all 'the vermin kind; such as weasels, foumarts, badgers, 'rats, mice, etc. It is fierce, keen, and hardy; and

[1] See *History of Quadrupeds*. Thomas Bewick, Newcastle-on-Tyne, 1790.

'in its encounters with the badger sometimes meets 'with very severe treatment, which it sustains with 'great courage and fortitude. A well-trained veteran 'dog frequently proves more than a match for that 'hard-bitten animal. There are two kinds of 'terriers: *the one is rough, short-legged, long-backed, 'very strong, and most commonly of a black or 'yellowish colour mixed with white,*[1] the other is 'smooth, sleek, and beautifully formed, having a 'shorter body, and more sprightly appearance; it is 'generally of a reddish-brown colour, or black with 'tanned legs; and is similar to the rough terrier 'in disposition and faculties, but inferior in size, 'strength, and hardiness.'

It will be remembered that Sir Walter Scott, in his notes to *Guy Mannering*, speaks of James Davidson's terriers as being 'yellow or greyish black.'

The written account of the 'rough terrier' thus given by Bewick is a fair description of the terriers owned by James Davidson, Hindlee, and his hunting companion, Ned Dunn, Whitelee, both of whom are known to have procured their terriers from the Allans and others of the Border 'Mugger' tribes. I must however admit that the engraving of Bewick's terrier represents a most wretched

[1] The italics are mine.

curly-tailed mongrel, and I therefore here give, by the kind permission of the Duke of Buccleuch, an etching of the head of a terrier which belonged to Henry, third Duke of Buccleuch, taken from a picture painted in 1770 by Gainsborough, to show the the real Border type of terrier of a century ago. There can be little doubt that the old Border terriers of this type formed the raw material from which has sprung the Dandie Dinmont.

Mr. Robert White of Newcastle-on-Tyne says,[1] in speaking of the race of terriers possessed by James Davidson, Hindlee: 'I have seen the 'genuine breed long ago at Ned Dunn's of the 'Whitelee at the head of Redesdale. Among 'common dogs they were something like the Black 'Dwarf among men, long-bodied animals with 'strong short legs, wiry-haired, and at the first look 'not unlike a low four-footed stool, such as I have 'seen in houses in the south of Scotland forty 'years ago. They were sent in to the fox when 'he was earthed, and fought him there.'

'A Border Sportsman' (probably James Scott, Newstead, another hunting companion of James Davidson in his youth), in the letter in the *Field* before referred to,[2] says, 'The real pure original 'Pepper and Mustard race, as bred by young

[1] See *Horæ Subsecivæ*, quoted *ante*. [2] See p. 26, *ante*.

Head of Terrier from Gainsborough's portrait of the Duke of Buccleuch, 1770

'Davidson, and as known by Sir Walter Scott, 'who has rendered it so famous in history, was 'a very long-bodied animal, short in the leg '(particularly so in front), with long head, and 'immensely strong jaws and teeth compared with 'the size of the creature; it had pendent ears 'like the hound or beagle, but had nothing of the 'hound or beagle in voice. In short, it was more a 'picturesque than a strictly handsome animal.' And again: 'These terriers were only ten to eleven 'inches high, and weighed only about from 13 lbs. 'to 18 lbs.; their coat was rough on the body, and 'hard and wiry, in what was called pencils; on the 'head soft and silky, and generally of a much lighter 'tint than that on the body; the legs and feet 'partook to a slight extent of the same soft silky 'hair as that on the head.'

Mr. Francis Somner, Kelso, thus describes the terrier bitch 'Nettle,' which, as before mentioned, he procured direct from Hindlee in or about the year 1820:—'Nettle was from the kennels of 'Dandie Dinmont direct. Her colour was a real 'pepper and salt, with the white, woolly, curly head, 'dark hazel eye, pendent ears, very long body upon 'short legs, with ankles, feet, and claws perfect. 'Weight eleven pounds. She was a game little 'thing, and of a very vicious nature, but from her 'small size she was never tried upon large vermin 'in case of her being destroyed.'

Of 'Old Pepper,' purchased from Allan, the basket-maker at Yetholm, and grandson of the original Piper Allan, Mr. Somner writes: '"Old Pepper" 'was purchased by me from a tinker in Yetholm 'famous for the purity of his breed of Dandie Din-'monts. He was a grandson of old Allan, the 'basket-maker in Holystone on the Coquet Water, 'and declared "Pepper" to be a true lineal descen-'dant of the famous dog "Hitchem," which it is said 'the Duke of Northumberland offered a liferent 'lease of a small farm for. The old basket-maker's 'reply was, "I wadna tak yer hale grund for '"him."' This anecdote has evidently the same origin as that referred to by Dr. John Brown in his *Horæ Subsecivæ*, mentioned at page 6.

Mr. Somner's famous dog 'Shem' was descended from both 'Nettle' and 'Old Pepper,' and regarding the other dogs in 'Shem's' pedigree he says: 'All the dogs used in this pedigree, besides 'possessing all the shapes and characteristics of 'the breed, before they were put together for the 'purpose of reproducing stock, were well tried 'with every sort of vermin, such as stoats, pole-'cats, cats, foxes, and badgers, etc. etc.'

Thus altogether we have a very distinct description given of the race of terriers as possessed by the Allans, Davidson, Dunn, etc., and further, the fact stated that Mr. Somner in selecting his terriers for breeding purposes took the greatest care only to use dogs of the original type possessed by Davidson. Mr. Somner's evidence as to this fact is very important at the present time, because it has been maintained by some that the type of the Dandie Dinmont of the present day has totally changed from what it was when possessed by James Davidson, Hindlee, and this chiefly because of cross-breeding. Mr. Somner's evidence however shows that the old breeders stuck fast to the original type and handed it down to their successors, while the pedigrees given in the Appendix are sufficient to show that the blood has been maintained pure.

'Stonehenge' lately departed from his primary theory that the Dandie Dinmont had originated in a cross between the old Scotch terrier and otter-hound or Welsh harrier, and stated that the original Dandie was really a pure terrier, while the modern Dandie was the result of a cross with the German Dachshund. The reader will here doubtless remember the theory referred to at page 3, that the Dandie Dinmont *originated* in a cross between terriers of the Dachshund type (brought by the Gypsies probably a couple of centuries ago from the continent of Europe) and the old-fashioned Border terrier. As regards the *origin* of the 'Pepper and Mustard' race, such a theory may or may not possibly be true, but as regards the contamination of the breed by such a cross in these latter times, 'Stonehenge' is most certainly mistaken. He writes in the *Field* of 5th May 1877 thus: 'Since my first acquaintance with the Dandie, 'pictorially and in the flesh, going back nearly half a 'century, a considerable elongation has taken place 'in the body as well as the ears of that dog,' and then, after giving an instance or two of short-eared and short-bodied terriers which were *reputed* Dandies over forty years ago, by way of proof (I should have said *instead* of proof), propounds the somewhat startling theory that the modern Dandie is the result of a cross with the Dachshund, from which the ears and body have been lengthened, and crooked legs and wide chests introduced, together with an entirely new obstinacy of disposition, which makes them almost, if not quite, uncontrollable when on a scent. Now I agree with 'Stonehenge' when he states that the Dandie was originally a '*terrier*' (it is a terrier still, and has never been anything else, but must not be confounded with spurious houndish-like dogs); but I demur altogether to his theory of a Dachshund cross,—

the more so as his theory was based on a *supposed* chance visit of the late Mr. E. Bradshaw Smith of Blackwoodhouse, Ecclefechan, accompanied by a favourite Dandie bitch, to the German Spas, during which, and in consequence of the designs or carelessness of a servant, a Dachshund had had access to this Dandie bitch,—a purely imaginary idea. In support of his theory, 'Stonehenge' refers to the portrait of a dog of Sir Walter Scott's, after referred to, and to his remembrance of a dog which belonged to a friend of his, and 'brought by him about forty-'five years ago from the Teviot district at consider-'able trouble and expense.'[1] Now, to say that from a supposititious chance visit, comparatively recently, to Germany, of one Dandie bitch, we are to account for the *whole race* of Dandie Dinmonts of the present day having long bodies, long ears, crooked fore-legs, broad chests, and obstinacy of temper—in short, for the bodily and mental qualities, of a breed of terriers being radically changed,—does seem a little startling. Many a long year, one would think, must pass before the Dachshund cross, if so obtained, could reach the Dandie Dinmont terrier as a *breed*, if indeed it could ever have reached it at all *appreciably*, for although Mr. Bradshaw Smith's kennel might speedily have been influenced by such

[1] See the *Field* of 5th May 1877.

a cross, it was but a favoured few who could obtain blood from the Blackwoodhouse kennels.

'Stonehenge's' Dachshund theory, however, as will be immediately noticed, was repudiated by Mr. E. Bradshaw Smith, whose authority 'Stonehenge' himself admits 'stands deservedly at the 'highest point.'[1] It was indeed fortunate that he pitched upon the Blackwoodhouse kennels as the channel conveying the *supposed* 'foreign' blood to the Dandie (although intensely annoying to Mr. Bradshaw Smith), for, had he made the statement generally, and without specifically stating the grounds for his belief, a mere baseless theory might, in course of time, have come to be looked on as a fact, simply because 'Stonehenge' was its author.

That crosses have taken place in many strains of so-called Dandie Dinmont terriers there can be no doubt; Dachshund, bull-terrier, otter-hound, all may have been employed by some breeders to produce the specimens exhibited by them at our dog-shows as 'Dandie Dinmont terriers.' Indeed, I believe that it was the exhibition of some of these cross-bred terriers in the early days of dog-shows that led to all the differences of opinion that have taken place regarding the true type of the Dandie

[1] *Dogs of the British Islands*, by J. H. Walsh ('Stonehenge'), 1882.

in the sporting journals. Often judged at first by those who had little or no experience of the pure breed, many mongrels took prizes as Dandies, and the public were thus erroneously taught to suppose that these were fine specimens of the historic race of 'Peppers and Mustards.' Thus the impure blood flourished for a time, and, being used at the stud, was largely disseminated. But granting that this is so, it will not prove that the pure breed has been altogether lost. On the contrary, if it be true that there do exist such cross-bred strains (and I grant that fact), there is equally no doubt that there are Dandies in existence whose blood has been untainted by any foreign cross, at any rate since the days of James Davidson of Hindlee,—lineal descendants of the original 'Peppers and Mustards' immortalised by Scott.

Here, for example, is the testimony of the late Mr. Eaglesfield Bradshaw Smith of Blackwood-house, whose Dandies, as I have already stated, were originally procured from undeniable sources, and who preserved the breed in all its purity for forty years (1841-1882). He says:[1]—'This state-'ment of "Stonehenge"' (viz. the Dachshund theory)

[1] See Mr. Eaglesfield Bradshaw Smith's letter in the *Field* of 17th November 1877.

'certainly implies a doubt as to the purity of my 'terriers. I, who have spared neither time, trouble, 'nor expense to obtain the breed and preserve it 'untainted, cannot allow this insinuation to pass 'uncontradicted. . . . Referring, then, to the in-'sinuation made by "Stonehenge" as above, I never 'bred terriers on the Continent.' He then states that, having kept these terriers since 1841, and having between that date and the date of his writing (1877) had more Dandies through his hands than any half-dozen fanciers, he felt competent to give a decided opinion on the article penned by 'Stonehenge,' although it 'be at variance with his remarks.'

He continues: 'In the first place, it seems to 'me an entire mistake on his (Stonehenge's) part 'that the Dandie Dinmont of the present day is 'longer in the body than formerly. My observation 'tends rather in the opposite direction.'

'Secondly, a strong characteristic of the breed 'has ever been tenacity of purpose, and I have only 'known two of my dogs which could be taught at 'command to leave the trail of either fox or rabbit; 'certainly it would be a hopeless task to prevent a 'Dandie Dinmont from engaging with a fox were 'an opportunity to offer.'

Mr. Smith further mentioned the kennels from which he had purchased his dogs originally, and stated that from these ancestors his dogs were 'purely and lineally descended.'

The editor of the *Field*, it is right to say, added this note to Mr. Smith's communication: 'We insert 'with pleasure the above letter, which, of course, 'upsets the attempt made in the original (Stone- 'henge's) article on the Dandie, to account for the 'long *ears* of the modern Dandie.' It will be noticed that Mr. Smith, however, did not specially speak about the *ears* of the original Dandie being as long as those of the modern Dandie, but of the *body*.

Notwithstanding this very clear and emphatic denial of Mr. Bradshaw Smith's, 'Stonehenge,' in his latest edition of *The Dog* (3d edition, 1879), disregards the above-quoted admission of the editor of the *Field*, and reiterates his Dachshund theory, quoting further in support of it a letter which appeared in the *Field* of 16th November 1878, from Mr. Matthias Smith of Leeds,[1] in which the allegation was made that even the reputedly purely bred Dandies of the present day are totally different from the original dogs possessed by James Davidson of Hindlee, and are nothing better than mongrels. In support of his argument, Mr. Matthias Smith mentioned (1.) that he had seen

[1] Mr. Matthias Smith's letter is only alluded to on account of the notice it has received from 'Stonehenge.'

the stuffed skin of a genuine Dandie Dinmont dog which Mr. Bradshaw Smith of Blackwood-house had owned, *viz.*, 'Dandie II.,' before mentioned; also the stuffed skin of Mr. P. S. Lang of Selkirk's 'Old Pepper;' and (2.) that he had seen at Abbotsford 'a portrait of a Dandie Dinmont, 'painted by the late Sir Edwin Landseer, which 'dog, when alive, belonged to the late Sir Walter 'Scott.' Wherein the difference between the original Dandie Dinmont (as exemplified by these stuffed skins and the Abbotsford painting) and the modern Dandie lay, Mr. Matthias Smith did not, however, explain, and, although repeatedly called upon to do so, he simply reiterated the statement without offering further explanation or proof. The question, therefore, as the editor of the *Field* in a foot-note put it, 'lies in a nutshell. If he can prove his state-'ments, it appears to us that his case is a strong 'one; while, on the contrary, if they are disproved, it 'falls to the ground. . . . The matter should hinge on 'the truth or falsehood of his plain and straight-'forward statements,' etc. Mr. Matthias Smith, having made 'his plain and straightforward state-'ments,' however, as before mentioned, rested content, and offered no further explanation or proof by way of support. All the leading fanciers and others interested in the Dandie Dinmont terrier,

"Old Pepper"

however, not only challenged the statements of 'Stonehenge' and Mr. Matthias Smith, but demonstrated that the slender proof adduced by them was untrustworthy. For instance, Mr. Bradshaw Smith, the owner of the stuffed skin at Blackwoodhouse, wrote:[1] 'I regret much that my stuffed dogs were 'shown to Mr. Matthias Smith of Leeds, as, though 'they were splendid specimens in life, having been 'badly stuffed they can convey no notion now of 'what they actually were. The larger of the two '(the dog) is probably the one referred to by Mr. 'Matthias Smith of Leeds. It is a complete botch, 'and stands under a table so as not to attract attention.' So much for Mr. Matthias Smith's conclusions regarding the stuffed specimen at Blackwoodhouse of the undoubted breed. Regarding the stuffed skin of Mr. Lang's 'Old Pepper,' I leave fanciers to judge for themselves, by examining the etching placed opposite this page, and which has been made from the stuffed skin itself. As to the Abbotsford picture, there is absolutely no proof whatever that it was, or was ever meant to pass for, the portrait of a pure Dandie Dinmont terrier.

The only person whose opinion carried any authority, who supported 'Stonehenge' and Mr. Matthias Smith in their contention, was the late

[1] *Field*, 28th December 1878.

Mr. Alexander J. Adie of Linlithgow, who wrote :[1] 'The description by "Stonehenge" of the original 'dogs agrees with what I recollect of them more 'than fifty years ago, and I have kept them ever 'since. My school vacations were spent at the 'house of a friend near Kelso, and there I made 'my first acquaintance with a Dandie, Matcham by 'name. He belonged to Lady Diana Scott, Rose-'bank, Kelso, and, to the best of my recollection, in 'all respects resembled "Stonehenge's" description 'of the old kind; an active, well-proportioned dog, 'with small, thin ears close to his cheeks, straight 'legs, and good feet, well suited for a long day's 'work. . . . Afterwards I had several of Mr. 'Davidson's breed given me by my friend; they 'were all much alike in shape, and very unlike the 'prize dog of the present day. I was able to keep 'the old type, with fine eyes, small ears, and straight 'legs, until about fifteen years since; but the cross 'breed then came to me, and I have not been able 'to get back to what I consider the true one. . . . 'The old kind had fine tempers, not much given to 'fight; but I had two dogs killed stone-dead, in a 'private battle, although they had never been 'allowed to fight when there was any one at hand

[1] See *Dogs of the British Islands*, by J. H. Walsh ('Stonehenge'), 4th Edition, 1882.

'to separate them. Having so long been in possession of Dandies, I was glad to see an accurate 'description of the old race, which, to my mind, 'were nicer dogs than what we see in the present 'long-eared, bent-legged prize ones. Indeed, the 'first time I saw them at a dog-show the thought 'immediately occurred to me that these are not 'Dandies.'

From Mr. Adie's description of his terriers I fear that they cannot have been of the true Pepper and Mustard race (although doubtless allied to it), for while his letter does carry some weight at first sight, and may be true as regards many of the dogs exhibited in the early days of dog-shows here and there as Dandies, his opinion loses all value when weighed against the evidence of such old breeders as the late Mr. John Stewart Lyon of Kirkmichael, the late Mr. Nicol Milne of Faldonside, the late Mr. E. Bradshaw Smith of Blackwoodhouse, Mr. James Aitken, Edinburgh, and other experienced and well-known breeders, who have described to us the points of the pure breed, and who maintain that they have in breeding stuck not only to the lineal descendants of the pure race of 'Peppers and Mustards,' but have bred to the old lines and adhered to the old type. Apart from the evidence to be found in the Blackwoodhouse records, is it conceivable that such old and ardent fanciers, who appreciated to the full the historical interest of the breed, would stain their kennels with the taint of any cross-blood? I confidently say, No, and I would refer to the anecdote told on page 47 of old John Stoddart of Selkirk, as a direct proof to the contrary.

Further, in Appendices IV. and V. will be found the pedigrees of two existing Dandie Dinmont terriers, which have been inserted to show that two of the best-known prize-winners of the present day are 'lineal descendants of the pure race of Peppers 'and Mustards.' Thus the *dicta* laid down by 'Stonehenge,' Mr. Matthias Smith, and Mr. Adie, being altogether at variance with the statements of all the old, experienced, and well-known breeders, and being, besides, totally unsupported by any evidence, must be dismissed as unworthy of serious consideration.

But, although the blood may still be pure, may not the *type* have changed? It is now more than sixty years since 'Dandie Dinmont' was gathered to his fathers, and half a century in the annals of dog history means a considerable period. Why, without going outside the pure stock left in the country at the date of James Davidson's death, the type of his famous little terrier might have become so changed by this time as to be beyond his recognition could he see them, although the blood would still be the same. Half a century of skilful or unskilful breeding will do wonders in altering the shapes and characteristics of such early-matured animals as dogs!

But has the type of the Pepper and Mustard race changed from what it was in Davidson's time? I think but little, and, if at all, probably for the better.

From the descriptions I have already quoted from Bewick, Mr. Robert White, Mr. Francis Somner, and Mr. James Scott, we have so far ascertained what the old breed were like. Besides this, I have referred to Lord Polwarth's 'Dandie,' which was a son of a dog and bitch given to Sir Walter Scott by James Davidson—'Dandie 'Dinmont' himself—as specimens of the genuine breed, and we may be sure 'Dandie' would not give anything but the best to Sir Walter. Of this dog Mr. E. Bradshaw Smith says, writing in 1843, and after he had seen the dog, that he was 'very 'handsome,' and the 'same as Sir Walter Scott's.' Now we know what sort of dog Mr. E. B. Smith considered 'very handsome.' He speaks also of Mr. Nicol Milne's 'Jenny,' J. Stoddart's 'Old 'Dandie,' 'Podgy II.' (whose portrait is here given, and which is just the stamp of terrier to catch the eye of a good judge at the present time),[1] and others of his own breeding, as 'very handsome,' and from these dogs his stock was descended.

Altogether there was ample evidence as to the appearance of the pure race of Dandie Dinmont terriers, in the statements of Mr. Francis Somner, Mr. James Scott, Mr. E. B. Smith, Mr. James Aitken, and other veteran breeders, but, in consequence of the constantly recurring controversies, there was formed in 1876 'The Dandie Dinmont 'Terrier Club,' with the object of 'at once and for 'ever' settling the points of the breed. For this purpose all the most noted breeders of the Dandie and others interested were invited to give their views as to the appearance and points of the breed. The result of the deliberations of the Club (which had Lord Melgund and Mr. E. Bradshaw Smith respectively as President and Vice-President) is contained in the admirable 'Standard of Ex-'cellence' with which I close this chapter, as it is in its way a most accurate description of the original Pepper and Mustard or Dandie Dinmont terrier.

[1] This portrait of 'Podgy II.' is copied from a clever sketch made at Blackwoodhouse on 29th May 1863 by Mr. J. C. W. Douglas, and is referred to in the *Field* of 30th November 1878. The landscape is Mr. W. Hole's work. Of Podgy II. Mr. E. B. Smith writes in January 1876: 'Podgy II. was a dark bluish grey, with a fine silky head. She was the 'image of her mother, Podgy I.; they could scarcely be distinguished one 'from the other, and were both particularly handsome.'

"Podgy II."

THE DANDIE DINMONT TERRIER CLUB'S 'STANDARD OF EXCELLENCE.'

Head.—Strongly made and large, not out of proportion to the dog's size, the muscles showing extraordinary development, more especially the maxillary. *Skull* broad between the ears, getting gradually less towards the eyes, and measuring about the same from the inner corner of the eye to back of skull as it does from ear to ear. The forehead well domed. The head is *covered* with very soft silky hair (which should not be confined to a mere top-knot, and the lighter in colour and silkier it is, the better). The *Cheeks*, starting from the ears proportionately with the skull, have a gradual taper towards the *Muzzle*, which is deep and strongly made, and measures about three inches in length, or in proportion to skull as three is to five. The Muzzle is covered with hair of a little darker shade than the top-knot, and of the same texture as the feather of the fore-legs. The top of the Muzzle is generally bare for about an inch from the back part of the nose, the bareness coming to a point towards the eye, and being about one inch broad at the nose. The nose and inside of *Mouth* black or dark coloured. The *Teeth* very strong, especially the canine, which are of extraordinary size for such a small dog. The canines fit well into each other, so as to give the greatest available holding and punishing power, and the teeth are level in front, the upper ones very slightly overlapping the under ones. [Many of the finest specimens have a 'Swine-mouth,' which is very objectionable, but it is not so great an objection as the protrusion of the under jaw.]

Eyes.—Set wide apart, large, full, round, bright, expressive of great determination, intelligence, and dignity; set low and prominent in front of the head; colour, a rich dark hazel.

Ears.—Large and pendulous, set well back, wide apart, and low on the skull, hanging close to the cheek, with a very slight projection at the base, broad at the junction of the head, and tapering almost to a point, the fore-part of ear tapering very little—the taper being mostly on the back part, the fore-part of the ear coming almost straight down from its junction with the head to the tip. They are covered with a soft straight brown hair (in some cases almost black), and have a thin feather of light hair starting about two inches from the tip, and of nearly the same colour and texture as the top-knot, which gives the ear the appearance of a *distinct point.* The animal is often one or two years old before the feather is shown. The cartilage and skin of the ear should not be thick, but rather thin. Length of ear from three to four inches.

Neck.—Very muscular, well developed, and strong, showing great power of resistance, being well set into the shoulders.

Body.—Long, strong, and flexible; ribs well sprung and round, chest well developed and let well down between the fore-legs; the back rather low at the shoulder, having a slight downward curve and a corresponding arch over the loins, with a very slight gradual drop from top of loins to root of tail; both sides of back-bone well supplied with muscle.

Tail.—Rather short, say from eight inches to ten inches, and covered on the upper side with wiry hair of darker colour than that of the body, the hair on the under side being lighter in colour, and not so wiry, with a nice feather about two inches long, getting shorter as it nears the tip; rather thick at the root, getting thicker for about four inches, then tapering off to a point. It should not be twisted or curled in any way, but should come up with a regular curve like a scimitar, the tip, when excited, being in a perpendicular line with the root of the tail. It should neither be set on too high nor too low.

When not excited it is carried gaily, and a little above the level of the body.

Legs.—The fore-legs short, with immense muscular development and bone, set wide apart, the chest coming well down between them. The feet well formed, ***and not flat***, with very strong brown or dark-coloured claws. Bandy legs and flat feet are objectionable, but may be avoided—the bandy legs by the use of splints when first noticed, and the flat feet by exercise, and a dry bed and floor to kennel. The hair on the fore-legs and feet of a blue dog should be tan, varying according to the body colour from a rich tan to a pale fawn; of a Mustard dog they are of a darker shade than its head, which is a creamy white. In both colours there is a nice feather, about two inches long, rather lighter in colour than the hair on the fore-part of the leg. The hind legs are a little longer than the fore ones, and are set rather wide apart, but not spread out in an unnatural manner, while the feet are much smaller; the thighs are well developed, and the hair of the same colour and texture as the fore ones, but having no feather or dew-claws; the whole claws should be dark, but the claws of all vary in shade according to the colour of dog's body.

Coat.—This is a very important point; the hair

should be about two inches long, that from skull to root of tail a mixture of hardish and soft hair, which gives a sort of crisp feel to the hand. The hard should not be wiry; the coat is what is termed pily, or pencilled. The hair on the under part of the body is lighter in colour and softer than that on the top. The skin on the belly accords with the colour of the dog.

Colour.—The colour is pepper or mustard. The pepper colour ranges from a dark bluish black to a light silvery grey, the intermediate shades being preferred, the body colour coming well down the shoulder and hips, gradually merging into the leg colour. The Mustards vary from a reddish brown to a pale fawn, the head being a creamy white, the legs and feet of a shade darker than the head. The claws are dark, as in other colours. [Nearly all Dandie Dinmont terriers have some white on the chest, and some have also white claws.]

Size.—The height should be from eight to eleven inches at the top of shoulder. Length from top of shoulder to root of tail should not be more than twice the dog's height, but preferably one or two inches less.

Weight.—From 14 lb. to 24 lb.; the best weight as near 18 lb. as possible. These weights are for dogs in good working order.

The relative values of the several points in the Standard are as follow :—

Head,	10	Coat,	15
Eyes,	10	Colour,	5
Ears,	10	Size and weight,	5
Neck,	5	General appearance,	5
Body,	20		
Tail,	5	Total,	100
Legs and feet,	10		

CHAPTER IV.

The Standard of Excellence alone is not conclusive as to what is or is not a Dandie—Pedigree, as a proof of true breeding, and its value to the breeder—The outward characteristics of the pure breed as recognised by the old breeders, and laid down in the Standard of the Dandie Dinmont Club, amplified.

THE Standard of Excellence thus drawn up by the Dandie Dinmont Terrier Club, while in a way an exhaustive analysis of the points of the Pepper and Mustard race, is not however in itself sufficient to determine what is or is not a Dandie, for by skilful breeding it is possible to produce (and there have been produced) dogs which seemingly answer to the Standard's description, but which, nevertheless, are most certainly *not* Dandies. When I say this I anticipate the expostulations which many will make against an opinion which seems to involve a paradox. I will, however, endeavour to explain my meaning.

Although, as I have said, you may have a dog answering in its points fairly well to the Standard's description of a Dandie, yet that dog may want altogether the true Dandie 'character.' Here, again, I think I hear the exclamation, 'Character! 'what is that?' and I may at once admit that I cannot in so many words inform my readers what 'character' is, although I hope to be able indirectly to convey my meaning.

For example, the distinction to the eye of a connoisseur in art between a genuine painting by one of the old masters and a copy executed by a skilful copyist is at once apparent, although to the eye of one not skilled in art the copy is as good as the original, nay, it is possibly thought better! The difference between original and copy however exists as unmistakably to the trained eye as the difference between chalk and cheese is to the eye of a grocer, yet who could write down a formula which would enable any one to distinguish between the genuine and the clever copy? The difference exists, yet is indescribable, and, like distinctions of style in literature, and such occult subjects, to be understood and appreciated must be studied under the best authorities, and the one carefully compared with the other.

Now the case of the Dandie Dinmont terrier is much like that of works of art, for it is possible to have two terriers to the eye of the uninitiated apparently identical, yet the expert pronounces one to be a Dandie, the other only a clever copy. It is indeed occasionally difficult to lay one's finger on any particular point in a dog, and say, 'Here the impure 'blood is to be seen cropping out;' but while even the expert may be unable to do this, yet he will confidently quote the lines, 'The reason why I 'cannot tell, but I don't like thee, Dr. Fell,'—an admittedly insufficient reason, but one which nevertheless may be sound. The proof, however, which can be offered in support of the expert's dictum as to the indescribable 'something' (which he sees plainly enough), and which constitutes the one to be a pure-bred Dandie, and the other a mongrel, is that of 'pedi-'gree.' And here, too, I desire not to be misunderstood, for I quite sympathise with those who ask what manner of proof it is to say, in support of an assertion of the purity of any particular dog as a Dandie, that he is by so-and-so's 'Jock' out of somebody else's 'Jenny,' and so on *ad infinitum*, when nothing is known of either 'so-and-so,' or the 'somebody else,' and still less of their dogs. But when one can show such pedigrees as had the terriers of Mr. Somner, Mr. James Scott, Mr. E. Bradshaw Smith, and other old and known breeders, and which you can trace back in known hands direct to James Davidson, Hindlee, then I do say that 'pedigree' is invaluable, and supplies the proof to support the 'character' seen in the really pure-bred Dandie. Such pedigrees, I say, are invaluable to the breeder, for by them he knows when mating the parents what to expect in the produce, for the pedigreed parent is the result of long years of patient and systematic breeding, and has the type of a long list of carefully selected ancestors indelibly stamped upon its form. The effect of 'pedigree,' *i.e.* purity of race, in breeding with mixed blood is, that to a great extent the characteristics of the pure-bred parent will be reproduced in the offspring, for it has a fixed type to throw to, while the mongrel, having half a dozen varieties in its composition, has not the same power of individual reproduction.

Breeding from unpedigreed parents, however excellent these may individually be as specimens of the breed they purport to be, is entirely a lottery, and the produce may resemble any one of the half-dozen different types of which it is composed. With parents of good pedigree it is quite otherwise, for even if they are not individually as handsome in appearance as the 'pretenders,' yet they will to a certainty produce offspring showing the characteristics of the pure breed to which they belong.

Thus to the breeder of the Dandie Dinmont terrier (as with any other pure-bred stock) a genuine pedigree is invaluable. In the show ring, of course, it is quite otherwise, for *there* a dog must be judged entirely by his appearance, the judge depending on his own eyes alone in forming an opinion on the merits of the animals brought before him in competition.

To get back, however, to the question of what is the true 'character' of the Dandie Dinmont (which is to be observed in certain outlines and details of formation, quality, and texture of coat, style of top-knot, cast of countenance or 'expression,' carriage, and general bearing, all of which to the eye of the expert conveys much, and enable him to draw the distinctions between the pure and the spurious Dandie), the following supplemental remarks (taking the points in the order of the 'Standard') may perhaps be not out of place.

Head.—While the skull should be round and well domed, it should not peak at the back in the fashion of a blood-hound's head. When I see in a terrier, purporting to be a Dandie, great development of the occipital protuberance, I think of 'Stonehenge' and his Dachshund theory. Some have insisted that the Dandie should have a very large and broad head. Mr. James Scott of Newstead on this point wrote :[1] 'The pure Dandie has 'not at all a broad head; the head is a large one,

[1] See the *Field* of 4th December 1869.

'but it is rather a long one than a broad one.' Mr. Bradshaw Smith says:[1] 'The head handsome and 'large, but not out of proportion to the size of the 'dog. Many mongrels have much larger heads than 'the pure-bred Dandie Dinmont;' and it is to be remembered that the head-covering, or, as it is technically called, the 'top-knot,' makes the head appear larger than it really is. The head, though largish, must not be heavy and dull-looking, but be of smart *terrier* formation.

Muzzle and Mouth.—The muzzle should be rather deep than broad (but not heavy-looking), and should start from the skull distinctly,—not tapering too much from its base towards the nose. Over- and under-shot 'mouths' are, unfortunately, not uncommon among Dandies, and appear in strains of the 'bluest blood,' and although very objectionable, when the fault is so great as to spoil the contour of the head, or detract from the utility of the terrier as a workman, are not to be considered any sign of impurity of breed, uneven mouths having been known in the breed from the earliest times.[2] Breeders, however, would do well if they would avoid as much as possible very defective mouths, and 'put down' such pups

[1] See Mr. E. B. Smith's notes on the D. D. Terrier Club's Standard of Excellence, in *The Country* of 1st June 1876.

[2] *Vide* the case of 'Schan' from Hindlee, mentioned at page 45.

as do not promise to have comparatively good mouths; for if the pup is allowed to grow up to dog's estate it goes against one's heart to destroy an animal which probably, except as to its mouth, is a fine specimen of its race, and may also be one which by that time has acquired a hold on its owner's affections. A slight pig-jaw does very occasionally grow more level as the pup grows older, but as a rule it shows more as the pup grows, and so to avoid all temptation to breed from a 'piggy' let the uneven-mouthed pup be destroyed as soon as the defect (if very bad) is discovered. Jaws, if much 'under-hung,' are, if possible, worse than a 'swine-mouth,' and when very bad are apt, if accompanied with a narrow skull and short muzzle, to give a mean look to the wearer's face. The remark as to putting down badly swine-mouthed pups applies also in the case of 'under-hung' pups, when the fault is great; but I may here remark that in many cases defective mouths cannot be noticed until the pup is some weeks old, and in under-hung mouths, when the fault is slight, often not until some months old. Regarding this vexed question of level mouths, I may perhaps be allowed to say here that it has always seemed to me to be absurd that a dog should be passed over in the show ring solely on account of his being *slightly* (often very slightly) over- or under-shot. If the defect is so slight as not to impair the dog's usefulness as a workman, then it seems to me that the fault should only count against him in the same way as a curled tail, or badly shaped or carried ears, or pale eyes, would do, viz., so many points should be deducted for the defect. On the other hand, if the defect is so bad as to prevent the dog being able to hold and kill vermin, then, and then alone, should he be passed over, whatever may be his other good points. I may say that I have seen dogs, some slightly over- and others slightly under-shot, that yet could hold and kill vermin quite as well as any level-mouthed terrier could do. Other points however being equal, the level-mouthed dog should certainly be placed before the uneven-mouthed dog in the show ring.

The large size of the teeth of the Dandie in comparison to his size is very noticeable. The face and jaws, however, are not like that of a crocodile, as once wrote a Birmingham judge,[1] but the development of the muscles which move the lower jaw is large, and the holding and punishing power of the jaws of a Dandie are therefore very considerable. I would point out, however, that a *fine* muzzle does not *necessarily* imply weakness of jaw. Strength of jaw and punishing power come from the muscles

[1] See Mr. C. Collins' letter in the *Field* of 9th January 1869.

which lie further back, and do not lie in the muzzle itself. Hence strong muscular development, combined with a comparatively fine muzzle, gives greater holding and punishing power than where the jaws are merely large and the muscles which work them deficient.

The inside of the mouth should be black, or at any rate dark-coloured, and free from light spots.

The *Nose* should be black. 'Cherry' or flesh-coloured noses, however, were occasionally seen in the breed, I have ascertained, long ago, although always scarce. Some breeders have maintained that the 'Cherry' nose was introduced about the year 1840 through a certain alleged 'Russian' dog. Of the breeding of this dog nothing is known, but Mr. Somner, writing in 1849, says, he 'belonged 'to a person in Dalkeith, weight 18 lbs. and re-'puted very game. He caught an otter in the Esk, 'pulled him out of the water, and worried him in 'presence of at least 1000 (*sic*) individuals. He 'was a beautiful dog, and resembled the Dandie 'Dinmont breed very much.' I suspect that this dog had more of the old-fashioned Bedlington in his composition than anything 'Russian,' although probably he was a '*travelled*' dog,—in the sense that he had made a voyage abroad.

Mr. James Aitken, Edinburgh, informs me he remembers seeing this dog at Melrose long ago; that he was not unlike a liver-coloured Bedlington, with pale salmon-coloured eyes and red nose; and that a lot of his progeny, which were very game, got about the country-side. There is no doubt that the so-called 'Russian' was used by some breeders to cross with their terriers, but both Mr. Somner and Mr. Aitken assured me that all the leading breeders had been very careful to avoid using any dogs in breeding which were tainted with this cross.

Hugh Purves, Leaderfoot, on the other hand, attributed the appearance of chestnut Dandies with flesh-coloured noses to the use of red bull-dogs in crossing Dandies for the purpose of getting determination and staunchness in taking punishment from large vermin, but here again I find that Mr. James Scott, Mr. James Aitken, and other old breeders, repudiate any taint of bull blood, saying that, while they know some breeders tried such a cross, it was a great mistake, did no good to the breed, and was, therefore, studiously avoided by careful breeders.

There seems altogether to be no doubt (indeed there is proof) that now and again, and apart from any occasional possible crossings with such as the 'Russian' or bull-dog, these chestnut or liver-coloured Dandies, with pale eyes and flesh noses, did appear in even the purest strains, but they always seem to have been scarce, and, not being appreciated, were seldom bred from, or kept. In all probability this chestnut colour was merely a successful effort of Nature to throw back to the common stock from which have sprung, as I believe, both the Dandie Dinmont and the Bedlington Terrier. That these terriers should have had a common origin may sound unwelcome to some ears, but there seems to be no reason to doubt it. The early history of both breeds traces back to the Coquetdale district, and the points of resemblance between these now totally distinct breeds was very much stronger long ago than now. The Bedlington of early times was of a stouter build and somewhat lower in the leg than his modern representative, and altogether more closely resembled the Dandie; but speed being considered desirable, breeders have gradually departed from the old type, and inclined to a lighter-built dog. Further, while there may still exist plenty pure-bred Bedlingtons, this desire for speed has in many cases resulted in the breed being crossed by the Northumbrian and Durham miners with 'whippets,' and other speedy dogs, for coursing and racing purposes, which has greatly helped to alter its original type. The 'liver' or chestnut colour has always been a prevailing and accepted colour in the Bedlington race, but this colour has nowadays almost entirely disappeared from the Dandie Dinmont family, where it was never appreciated nor encouraged. I do, however, know of an instance or two where the chestnut colour has comparatively recently cropped out,—only, however, to be consigned to the pail.

The colour of the nose of the Dandie Dinmont should therefore be black.

The ridge of the muzzle, for about an inch behind the nose and towards the eyes, should look bare of hair; the bare part being darkish in colour corresponds with the dark ears, the darkish shade under the eyes, and the deep tint of the eyes themselves, —and gives a gipsy game expression to the face. If the muzzle is examined closely, however, it will be found that while the ridge *looks* bare of hair, it is really covered with very short fine hair of a somewhat different texture from that on the jaws. No amount of faking can produce the real Dandie muzzle, and a judge of the breed should be able to identify this characteristic of the breed at a glance.

The *Eyes* should be full and expressive,—the colour of the iris being a *dark* hazel (if possible, so dark as to seem black at a little distance), and this whatever the colour of the dog, excepting always in the case of the 'Chestnuts' before referred to, whose eyes are of a pale yellowish colour. With this exception, the eyes should invariably be dark hazel. Mr. Nicol Milne of Faldonside used to insist 'on 'the large dark eye (not the tawny light hazel so 'commonly met with in many so-called Dandies) as 'a true characteristic of the genuine breed.'[1] The favourite eye is, I am bound to confess, not so often seen nowadays as it should be.

Carelessness in breeding, however, doubtless largely accounts for this. I remember being much struck, on first seeing the Blackwoodhouse kennel, with the fine eyes the most of Mr. Smith's terriers had. The effect of the dark melting brown eye (capable however of flashing fire when roused) looking out from beneath a silvery-white 'top-knot' was charming.

The *Ears*, although certainly coming under the denomination of 'large and pendulous,' should *not* be like to a hound's in miniature. To a slight extent, indeed, they vary in size in individual specimens, some being smaller, while others are larger. The ear to be aimed at, however, is as described in the Standard. The too small ear seldom hangs properly, while too large an ear

[1] See *The Field Quarterly Review* for 1870, p. 10.

gives a houndish look. The 'feather,' when abundant, sometimes makes the ears look larger and longer than they really are, but when there is little 'feather' (which I greatly prefer), and the ear is covered only with short dark hair (which gives the ear the appearance of velvet), but having a nice white 'feather' at the tip, it should not appear either very large or very long. The chief fault in many modern dogs is the breadth of the ear towards the tip. The true ear should be longish, but not very broad, narrowing sharply towards the tip, lying close in to the cheek, and set low on the head, and, while the front edge should run in a line 'straight down from its junction with the head to the tip,' and not in a semicircular curve, 'the taper being mostly on the back part,' the ear should not hang *quite* straight down, but should incline slightly forwards towards the eye.

The illustration given of Mr. J. B. Richardson's 'Shem' shows the correct type of the head of the Dandie Dinmont terrier.[1]

The *Tail*, although carried '*houndily*,' should *not* be a hound's tail. It should be in character more 'Scotch terrier' than hound. It should be strong and thick at the root, coming to a comparatively

[1] 'Shem' (whelped 1870, died 1883) was dark grey and tan, with light silky head; weight 19 lb.

fine point at the tip. Grasping the tail in one hand at the root, and placing the other hand immediately behind the first, the difference in the thickness of the parts of the tail in the two hands should be very noticeable, the portion in the hand nearest the tip being very much thinner than that in the hand next the root. The hair on the tail should be perhaps a little harder than that on the body, that on the upper side being similar to or darker in colour than that on the back, while on the under side it should be tan. The tail should be set on neither too high nor too low on the back, and be carried gaily like 'the sabre of my sire.' The shorter and straighter the tail is, the better.

The Legs.—The fore-legs should certainly be short and strong, but care should be taken in this, as in all other points, that this characteristic should not be exaggerated. If the fore-legs are reduced to mere 'stumps' (as I have seen them), the dog can hardly get about, and his use as an all-round vermin dog is much curtailed. Mr. Nicol Milne of Faldonside did not object to his dogs being 'a 'little leggy,' which meant, I take it, that he did not think badly of a dog if it were a trifle 'leggy,' *for a Dandie*, but which otherwise showed good breeding. Some difference of opinion formerly existed as to whether the fore-legs should be bent or straight.

Mr. F. Somner of Kelso says they 'should be bent 'inward at the ankle, and the toes turned out,' considering this to be 'one of the natural points of a 'Dandie, which is intended to work like a mole 'underground, pushing the earth on either side 'and leaving a passage for the body.' It is now, however, almost universally admitted that the straighter the fore-legs are the better, but it will be found, on examining the straightest-legged pure-bred Dandies that Mr. Somner's description is accurate, although the legs are not badly enough bent to constitute 'bandy' legs. The comparative broadness of the chest and shortness of the fore-legs necessitates a slight turning out of the feet, and from this cause badly-reared pups often get sadly twisted in the fore-legs. Utility in a vermin dog must never be lost sight of; and therefore the practically, though not literally, straight fore-legs with good bone and firm feet, is the most desirable form both for activity and for endurance in a hard day's work, and this form should be striven for in breeding.

The Coat.—This *is* 'a very important point,' as the Club rule puts it, and a never-ending source of distress to the Dandie breeder. It cannot be too distinctly understood that the Dandie Dinmont terrier is *not* a hard or broken-haired terrier, as some modern fanciers would appear to think. The Dandie is certainly a *rough-coated* dog, but the coat, while abundant, must not be too profuse. Too sparse a coat, on the other hand, is quite as bad a fault as (nay, worse than) a too abundant one. In fact, there is a mean in this particular, as in everything, and extremes in either direction are to be avoided. All this applies to the head-covering or 'top-knot,' as well as to the body coat. As the Club rule says, the hair on the back of the neck and upper part of the body should undoubtedly be a 'mixture of about two-thirds rather hard (but '*not* wiry), with one-third soft, linty, not silky, hair, 'which gives a sort of crisp feeling to the hand, 'and constitutes what old John Stoddart used to 'term a "pily" coat.' The coat should not 'shed' down the back, but should lie in 'pencils.' This is caused from the under coat being mostly soft hair, through which the longer and harder hair comes in tufts, the whole forming a coat capable of withstanding wet and cold, and drying rapidly after being wet.

Of late years there has been too great a tendency to try to breed the Dandie with an entirely hard coat, and specimens of this type are to be seen at shows whose coats are composed entirely of short hard hair, without any admixture or undergrowth of soft hair, and invariably accompanied by deficiency if not total absence of 'top-knot.' This is quite a mistake. The original breed had the mixed coat, and breeders should endeavour to stick to the old type. Reference to the etching of the head and neck of the famous 'May-day,' bred in 1836, and sold by Mr. D. M'Dougall, Cessford, to Mr. E. Bradshaw Smith, in whose possession she died, will exemplify this. 'May-day's' head[1] was unfortunately very badly stuffed, the true form and type of her head being completely lost, and to this has to be added nearly forty years' shrinkage, dust, and decay, all of which make the illustration here given of comparatively little worth, save for showing the style of coat of the old breed. The hair, however, remains as nature made it, and the illustration is given solely with the view of illustrating the style of 'top-knot,' etc., and not as showing the true type of the Dandie Dinmont's head.

Now, in the present day the advocates of the hard coat will think that 'May-day' shows too profuse a coat, and that the quality of the hair inclines too much to the soft side; but there she is

[1] In case of any misapprehension as to this illustration, I would explain that only the head and a few inches of neck exist in the stuffed remains of 'May-day.' Of these the artist has given an exact likeness; the rest of the illustration is imaginary, and filled in to give meaning and life to the stuffed remains.

as evidence that the coat laid down by the Dandie Dinmont Club is the correct texture.

In the matter of coat, however, it is well to remember that coats vary considerably even in the same litter, and thus a few generations of careful breeding will get either hard or soft coats, according to the wishes of the breeder, as any one experienced in such matters well knows. Thus too soft or too hard a coat must not be taken as of necessity implying *impurity of blood*, for the blood may be right enough, and the breeder be alone to blame, for his want of skill or opportunity in mating the progenitors of the too hard or too soft coated specimen. The original mixture of hardish and soft hair should always be aimed at by the breeder.

On the tail, as has been mentioned, the hair should be stronger or harder than on the back, while on the top of the head it should be very soft and silky. I once heard a noted modern exhibitor of the Dandie say, regarding the head-covering, 'Oh, 'bother the top-knot! What does a *terrier* want 'with a top-knot? Who cares whether it is there 'or not?' But a full head-covering (I don't much care for the term 'top-knot'), silvery white in colour and silky in texture, covering *the whole of the top of the head*, between the ears across, and from above the eyes (where the forelock grows, pointing forwards over the base of the muzzle), to the back of the skull lengthways, and *there ending abruptly*, like a 'coronet' (as Mr. F. Somner puts it), is an 'unco affset' to a Dandie, and is moreover typical of the true breed. One often sees the forelock 'plucked' or otherwise trimmed away from the top-knots of Dandies at shows, which, instead of improving, spoils the appearance of the dog. The 'top-knot' of the Dandie does not lie flat on the head, but is inclined to stand up in *slightly* twisted locks or 'pencils,' pointing slightly forwards in front.

One of the chief characteristics of the Dandie is to be seen in the full 'wig,' the dark lustrous eye, and the sharp outline of the bare muzzle, when the head is viewed in profile.

The hair on the ear should be short and velvety in texture, and if possible *dark* brown (the darker the better) in colour, with a thin feather of silvery white hair of similar texture to that of the 'top-'knot' fringing the tip.

Before closing my remarks on the *Coat* of the Dandie Dinmont I would allude, and just allude, to the disgraceful manner in which Dandies are sometimes trimmed for exhibition purposes. There is no doubt that the evil exists to a considerable extent, and Mr. James Locke of Selkirk, a well-known judge of Dandies, deserved great credit for speaking out so boldly on this point when writing in *The Kennel Gazette* of July 1883. Mr. Locke observes, 'Before closing I should like to 'add a few remarks on what appears to me to be a 'growing evil, and one which, if not stopped in time, 'may tend to frustrate most of the good brought 'about by shows and the Dandie Dinmont Club. I 'refer to dressing, brushing, trimming, or pulling, 'call it what you like. As one who has shown and 'bred this breed, I trust my remarks will be met in 'the same spirit in which they are offered : and, in 'the first place, I consider a dog ought to be shown 'as near as possible in working condition, as distin-'guished from a washed drawing-room condition. 'This being my standard, it becomes very difficult, 'or rather more difficult, to adjudicate on the dif-'ferent dogs brought before one if some are in hard-'working condition, some not touched, and evidently 'not having been worked, while others are beauti-'fully got up by hard brushing, pulling, etc.' I trust exhibitors will take these remarks to heart, and try to obtain the coat they desire their Dandies to have by *breeding better dogs*, and not by such paltry devices as pulling, shaving, etc.

The colour of the Dandie Dinmont may be either 'Pepper' or 'Mustard' of a lighter or darker shade, or a *mixture* of both.

The 'Pepper' and 'Mustard' colours are as mentioned in the Club's Standard of Excellence. There is, however, a colour of 'Pepper' of a brownish mousey shade, as also a variety combining both the Pepper and Mustard colours, in which case the 'saddle' is usually 'Pepper,' while the tan comes high up on the legs and body. The occurrence of the 'chestnut' colour, referred to at page 99, is so very occasional as not to be classed as a distinct variety.

Exactness in colour or markings is a 'fancy' point, and old breeders thought as much of the 'saddle-backs' as the perfect 'Peppers' or 'Mustards,' provided breeding, shapes, and gameness were otherwise good. Old John Stoddart's famous 'Dandie I.,' and his son 'Dandie II.,' were both 'saddle-backs,' but in these exhibition days this variety is out of fashion, and in close competition would, I fear, have to give way to the more decided colours, although a 'saddle-back' ought not to be passed over solely on account of colour. It is perhaps as well to have both the traditional colours of 'Pepper' and 'Mustard' kept distinct in the individual specimen, that is, that a dog should either be a 'Pepper' or a 'Mustard.' The 'top-knot' of the Pepper should be silvery white, while the Mustard's head-covering should be creamy white in colour.

The body colour should come well down on the shoulders and thighs, and the tan on the legs should be *palish* or fawn tan, and *not* the rich dark red mahogany tan of a Gordon setter.

The 'saddle-back' when two or three years old sometimes turns into a spurious 'Mustard,' the Pepper 'saddle' gradually dying out.

Dandie Dinmont pups when whelped are smooth in coat, the 'Peppers' being black and tan in colour, the more intense the black (viz., the freer from white or grey hairs) the darker the Pepper will probably turn out. Sometimes—although the occasions are rare—*Pepper* pups are whelped of a *silvery grey* and tan colour, which with age generally grows darker. 'Mustards' are whelped practically all tan colour (some being darker and others lighter in shade), there being little difference noticeable between the body colour and that on the legs, excepting that the hairs on the back and tail are usually more or less tipped with black. The ears, tail, and muzzle in Mustard pups are also often quite black, and if with this the crown of the head is a deep golden colour, the pup will usually grow into a fine Mustard. 'Saddle-backs' as pups are usually of a colour similar to the Peppers, but with more tan, the black body colour having a sort of fawn tint when seen in certain lights.

It may be added that a little white on the chest is common and permissible. The toes are also occasionally tipped with a little white, but this is most commonly seen in young puppies, and generally disappears in a few weeks or months. Too much white is however objectionable, and ought to be discouraged by avoiding breeding from dogs having too much white in their markings, tendencies of that sort taking every opportunity of reproducing themselves.

Size and Weight.—Considerable diversity of opinion exists as to the proper size and weight of the Dandie Dinmont terrier. This has arisen to a considerable extent from the great number of half-bred dogs which have been bred and sold to those who did not know the true breed, as pure Peppers and Mustards.

The favourite size in the original breed was however undoubtedly small. Mr. James Scott of Newstead wrote,[1] 'If we allow Mr. Davidson to decide 'the size and weight for us, none of them would 'exceed 16 lb. He was not at all chary in asserting 'that, if terriers were only made of the right stuff, 'they could not be too small.' Mr. Davidson's nephews wrote to the *Field*, in the course of the Dandie controversy, that the proper weight ran

[1] See the *Field* of 4th December 1869.

from 14 lb. to 18 lb. Mr. Francis Somner wrote, 'Weight of the male from 14 to 20 lb., and the 'female from 13 to 18 lb.' And again, 'I think '24 lb. weight too heavy. My average was 15 lb., 'and for every lb. less I valued them £1 more. 'A fox weighs from 11 lb. to 17 lb., and any 'practical sportsman will at once see that a dog 'of 24 lb. could not work the earths.' 'Drygrange 'Charlie,' the sire of 'Shem,' was only 12 lb., and 'Shem' 14 lb. Those kept by the Hon. G. H. Baillie of Mellerstain, writes Mr. James Scott,[1] 'were small, often 14 lb., seldom above '15 lb., and were most excellent at putting foxes 'out of drains. Some of them, small as they were, 'were unrivalled at badger. Those of Home of 'Carolside were also got from James Davidson, '. . . and were equally game and determined. 'Some of them only weighed 12 lb.'

The bitch 'Nettle,' which Mr. Somner obtained from Hindlee, weighed only 11 lb. I need not however multiply examples on this point, as the above are, I think, sufficient to indicate the favourite size of the original Dandie. It must not be, on the other hand, too hastily assumed that because a dog is a *trifle* on the heavy side of, say, 24 lb. weight, he must of necessity be impure, for in Dandies, as in

[1] See the *Field* of 16th October 1869.

all other animals, size and weight will vary a little in individuals. Care in breeding and rearing is required, as in all other points, to maintain anything like uniform weight. In the old days, undoubtedly, there were occasionally dogs of a somewhat large size bred, but these giants of their race, being too big for practical work, were of not much use, and so not highly valued, either as terriers or for the stud. In these modern times, when the great majority of Dandies are kept as companions, and not as mere vermin terriers, size does not matter so much, and consequently the 'big ones' have a greater chance than formerly of transmitting their size to posterity.

'Stonehenge' (writing in 1859) states that the weight varies from 18 lb. to 24 lb. according to the strain, 'but the original Dandie was a heavy 'dog,' a statement which is obviously erroneous in view of the particulars given above as to the favourite size with the sportsmen who used these terriers. There was indeed a strain of large terriers, similar in shape and colour to the pure Dandie, bred at Arks, Gateshaw, etc., but these were produced originally by crossing the pure Pepper and Mustard terrier with a big rough-haired 'otter terrier' bitch, and had no claim to be ranked as true Dandies, although resembling that breed in all but size. 'Dandie Dinmont' himself repudiated all but the small breed.

It stands to reason, I think, that a terrier which was used originally chiefly for bolting fox and otter must have been of a size small enough to allow him to go to ground freely, and no Dandie much over 18 lb. weight can do this.

The Dandie Dinmont Club therefore did wisely to restrict the *maximum* weight to 24 lb.,—the weight to be aimed at being 18 lb., which allows of a dog having plenty of bone and yet to be small enough for ordinary practical work. This refers to dogs in good *working* condition.

Mr. E. Bradshaw Smith, when remarking on the point of weight, dropped a useful enough hint to breeders, viz., that the heavy dogs 'are very useful 'to give bone, muscle, and stamina to the produce 'of the smaller ones,' but breeders must be careful not to impair the usefulness of the Dandie as a working terrier by breeding for too great bone and substance, as this makes the dog unwieldy in body, and slow in its movements, whereas the true Dandie should be active and smart on its legs and have a very flexible body. Had the Dandies of to-day more real work to do, the truth of this observation would at once be acknowledged, and the tendency to breed dogs of too great substance, and with too stout and short fore-legs, avoided. And here I would strongly impress upon the reader that the 'Dandie Dinmont' terrier is not, and never was, a 'fancy' terrier, but owes its fame solely to his qualifications as a *working* terrier. Breeders must therefore not allow themselves to be led away by 'fancy' points, and induced to breed terriers with what were originally desirable characteristics so exaggerated as to unfit them for practical work. A beauty exaggerated becomes a fault.

CHAPTER V.

The temperament of the Dandie Dinmont Terrier, and his capabilities as a vermin dog and as a companion.

HAVING discussed the outward appearance of the Dandie, let us now consider his temper, pluck, and capabilities as a vermin dog and as a companion.

The temper of the Dandie is as a rule unexceptionable. Usually a quiet, sedate, somewhat reserved dog, he is nevertheless a 'demon' when his blood is up. Much has been said and written for and against the pluck of the Dandie. My experience of the breed is that there is no more 'hard-bitten' terrier than a well-entered Dandie. But when will some people, when talking or writing on this point, keep in remembrance that sensible observation of 'Dandie Dinmont' to Brown:[1] 'A 'bonny terrier that, sir, and a fell chield at the 'vermin, I warrant him—*that is, if he's been weel 'entered, for it a' lies in that*'? And again: 'Beast 'or body, *education should aye be minded;* I have six 'terriers at home, Auld Pepper and Auld Mustard,

[1] See *Guy Mannering*.

'Young Pepper and Young Mustard, and Little 'Pepper and Little Mustard; . . . I had them a' 'regularly entered: first wi' rottens, then wi' stots 'or weasels, and then wi' the tods and brocks— 'and now they fear naething that ever cam' wi' a 'hairy skin on 't.'

Sir Walter knew what he was about when he penned these lines, and no advice could be sounder or more tersely put than '*Beast or body, education should aye be minded.*'

It must, however, be frankly admitted that many Dandies are 'shy' dogs when young, and the better bred they are the more this is sometimes the case. The reason is not far to seek. Every highly-bred animal is more 'nervous'—*i.e.* has nerves more highly strung or more sensitive—than coarser-bred animals, but, although more 'nervous,' it does not necessarily follow that at heart they are not just as plucky. Indeed, the reverse is usually the case. The difference between the temperament of a thorough-bred horse and that of a cart-bred horse will explain my meaning.

There is also no doubt of the fact that the really pure-bred Dandie of to-day is a considerably 'inbred' animal, which tends to cause this sensitiveness. Mr. Laverack may with his strain of setters have been able, by his great knowledge of his subject, for a time to inbreed to an extent previously unknown, but there is no room for doubt that inbreeding, unless conducted in a most intelligent manner (*i.e.* by crossing 'out' whenever any weakness shows), must end in degeneracy either of body or mind, or both. But while the Dandie is often shy when young, he seldom turns out so bashful when fully grown, if properly entered. 'Stonehenge' once wrote[1] that 'sometimes a 'Dandie pup of a good strain may appear not to be 'game at an early age; but he should not be parted 'with on that account, because many of them do not 'show their courage till nearly two years old, and 'then nothing can beat them; this apparent softness 'arising, as I suspect, *from kindness of heart*'—to which Dr. John Brown, in his usual happy manner, added,[2]—'a suspicion, my dear "Stonehenge," which 'is true, and shows your own "kindness of heart," 'as well as sense.' This kindly disposition of the Dandie, coupled with the fact that, if *wanted*, there is within him 'devil' enough to make him face anything, constitutes, to my mind, the very essence of what is required in a terrier. But there is one fault to this otherwise excellent character, for, *although he is often slow to rouse*, once roused, he is difficult

[1] See 'Stonehenge,' 1st Edition, 1859.
[2] *Horæ Subsecivæ*, quoted *ante*.

to restrain; the more punishment he gets, the more determined he becomes, and he never forgives 'an 'insult' nor loses an opportunity of avenging it. He also takes a 'deal of killing,' and one accustomed to the breed knows how often when a fight first arises the Dandie seemingly gets the worst of it, but waits quietly for the moment when the Dandie (which, most likely, has all this time been lying fighting on his back) shall arise, and proceed to demolish 'the enemy' with his powerful jaws, his antagonist having most likely only succeeded in filling his mouth with hair, and being completely 'blown.' The late Mr. Bradshaw Smith, in the letter to the *Field* of 17th November 1877, before referred to, wrote as to the temper and pluck of the Dandie, as follows,[1] viz: 'I consider the animal as naturally 'good-tempered, but, when once roused, he is ready 'to seize hold of anything within reach. When I 'first kept these dogs, I was ignorant of their 'extremely excitable nature, and had many killed 'from time to time in fights either in the kennels 'or at the entrance of rabbit-holes; in short, when 'once their blood is up, they become utterly un-'manageable. On this account, for years past '(though I keep a number), I do not allow more 'than one dog and one bitch in a kennel, but some-

[1] See the *Field* of 17th November 1877.

'times one dog and two bitches if very harmonious. 'The first I had worried, many years ago, was a 'beautiful little fellow, 14 lb. weight, bred by Mr. 'Kerss (Bowhill), from a sister of Stoddart's Old 'Dandie, and his own Old Pepper. He was killed 'in the night-time by another of my dogs, to my 'great annoyance. When I mentioned the circum-'stance to Mr. Kerss, he informed me that during 'the time this little animal belonged to him he had 'worried some of his, amongst the number a New-'foundland pup six months old. Yet it is by no 'means always the most excitable and pugnacious 'animal that stands the severest test, viz., to face 'alone two badgers at once, and fasten upon one of 'them, whilst the other in turn attacks him, as I 'have known very many to do. For my part, I 'prefer the dog who encounters his antagonist 'coolly, and without any fuss.'

Mr. Robert White, in his letters to 'Rab'[1] before alluded to, says, in speaking of the Dandies he remembered seeing at Ned Dunn's of the Whitelee, at the head of Redesdale, long ago: 'They seemed 'at first when out of doors to be shy, timid things, 'and would have slunk away from a fierce collie 'dog, but if he seized one of them, and the blood of 'the little creature got up, it just took a hold of him

[1] See *Horæ Subsecivæ*, by Dr. John Brown, quoted *ante*.

'in a biting place, and held on, never quitting till 'he found to his cost he had caught a tartar.' The *Border Sportsman*, before quoted, says:[1] 'The 'breed was certainly the most game and deter-'mined dog in existence. As proof of this I may 'mention that I have frequently seen one of these 'little creatures seize an otter while in the water, 'and go down with, and remain clinging to it for a 'length of time perfectly wonderful to witness.'

The character thus given to the Dandie by Mr. E. Bradshaw Smith, Mr. White, *Border Sportsman*, and others, is precisely what may be said of him at the present day, if properly entered, '*for it a' lies 'in that.*'

Pups should not be entered until they are about a year old, unless of a very forward disposition. Of course one often finds a plucky pup which will, with only its milk-teeth in, tackle a rat, but it is unfair, to my mind, to ask any young pup, before it is old enough to know what it all means, to face a savage old grey rat, however plucky the pup may be.

When the year-old pup, however, has been duly entered to rats, and understands what is wanted of him, he can be promoted to bigger 'game' as age and experience warrant, and opportunity offers.

In the olden time one could always get a badger,

[1] See the *Field* of 30th January 1869.

but the barbarous practice is now very properly vetoed. Still the terrier must be entered if he is to be of any use as a vermin dog,—nay more, if the *education* of a race of terriers is neglected for some generations, their capacities as vermin dogs may become greatly impaired, for there can be little doubt that mental as well as physical characteristics are hereditary, viz., transmissible from parent to offspring;—and if the pluck of your terriers has not been tested, then you run the risk of breeding from a coward, whose mild disposition may be inherited by his progeny;—and so, without being supposed to have any sympathies with the 'baiting' of any animal, I may give the following hint on the entering of the Dandie Dinmont to 'big game':—

The first thing to do when you get a new dog is to *make friends with him before you try his gameness* at vermin, as a dog, however plucky, is the better for the moral support of his greatest friend, his master, in taking severe punishment. It is a mistake to expect any terrier, however game, to tackle large vermin without first having been, as 'Dandie Dinmont' put it, '*regularly* entered: first 'wi' rottens, then wi' stots or weasels, and *then* wi' 'the tods and brocks,'—in other words, a dog must be gradually brought up to so high a standard of terrier proficiency as to face fox or badger without flinching, and cannot be rushed to the top of the tree all at once. Never try a dog at big vermin until he is from eighteen months to two years old. Remember a badger, fox, otter, or even an old 'tom' cat, is an awkward customer for even an experienced fighter, and inflicts very severe punishment on the dog. The badger usually bites the dog in the throat, not using his claws much. Foxes also bite very hard. The Dandie will however, when properly handled, face either fox or badger with the greatest determination. He is, indeed, particularly good under ground, where he seems to fear no foe, and will take punishment under ground that few other dogs would face.

As a general rule, all terriers require some training in the matter of going long to ground, for many a dog will 'go in' gamely above ground, which will hesitate to go up a long wet drain or earth, and tackle 'bogie' in the dark. Small size and a large heart are the two essentials for a good 'terrar' or 'earthe dogge,' and if only 'Barkis is willin' there is little difficulty in teaching to go freely to ground. The pure-bred Dandie has the qualifications necessary, and is second to none as a workman under ground. It also follows its game well in the water, to which it takes freely; and is equally good for river-side or covert hunting.

Mr. Somner, indeed, considers the Dandie Dinmont superior to all other terriers as a workman underground, maintaining that no other terrier shows such determination, or will take so much punishment underground from large vermin. In his large experience he has even occasionally seen young Dandies, which would face fox and badger in the most determined way *under ground*, while *above ground* they seemed somewhat shy of doing so. As an example of this peculiarity, he relates how on one occasion he had a young dog, which he was anxious to try at big vermin. One day his groom came to tell him that when coming homewards he had seen a fox go to ground in a drain at the side of the road. As it was not far off, Mr. Somner and his servant started for the spot, taking with them a spade, a sack, and the young dog. The groom had wisely placed a big stone on the mouth of the drain, which was quite a shallow one through to the adjoining field. The moment the stone was removed the terrier went in, and immediately was heard exchanging high words with the fox. After ascertaining the exact lie of the drain by putting down a long twig, Mr. Somner and his servant proceeded to dig down on the combatants. They reached the dog first, and digging down further on, the groom succeeded in 'tailing' the fox, and drew him out of the drain with the terrier hanging on to him in the most determined way. The fox was with some difficulty sacked and carried home. On the way home the groom remarked to Mr. Somner that he could not have believed that the young dog had so much pluck in him as to face a savage fox under ground. Mr. Somner took the opportunity to give the man a practical lesson on the nature of the Dandie.

Reaching home, he made the groom carry the fox into an empty byre. The young terrier was then brought into the byre, when the fox was turned out of the sack. The moment the great red wild brute was let loose—all ears, hair, and brush, bounding like an india-rubber ball up the walls in frantic endeavours to escape—the terrier's stern sank, and he could not be induced to look at the fox, far less to tackle him. Remember always that it was the first fox the dog had ever *seen*. The groom's astonishment and disgust were great. 'To think,' he said, 'that that dog was less than an hour ago 'fighting that very fox like a good 'un, and under 'ground too! I wouldn't ha'e believed it if I hadn't 'seen it mysel'.'

Mr. Somner then made the groom bring in the badger box,—a long nine foot wooden drain, which was covered over with litter, leaving only the mouth exposed. The fox was then chased round the byre, when he at once went to 'ground' in the badger box. Mr. Somner then took up the young dog in his arms, and fondled him, and carrying him to the mouth of the box set him down before it, holding him by the tail and encouraging him to go in, but always drawing him back again. The dog's eye kindled, and, with the knowledge that he was 'backed' by his master, he dashed into the box on being let go, and in a few minutes pulled out the fox by the 'scruff o' his neck.' The groom again 'wouldn't ha'e believed it if he hadn't seen it himsel'.'

From the above anecdote it will be seen that much depends on the owner of the dog how he turns out, and that there is a great deal in knowing the temper of a dog and how to handle him.

I should perhaps here say that, as a general rule, bitches will not stand so severe tests as dogs at big vermin.

Mr. Robert White, in writing to Dr. John Brown,[1] gives the following amusing account of what once happened to the veritable 'Dandie Dinmont' himself when entering some of his young terriers, which may not be out of place here :—

'Davidson wanted a cat from some of the cottages at a distance from Hindlee, that he might have the

[1] See *Horæ Subsecivæ*, quoted *ante*.

'young dogs tried upon it. One of his shepherds 'chanced to call at Andrew Telfer's house, where 'he saw *baudrons* sitting on the end of a dresser 'near the door; and the house being low and dark, 'he swept her into his plaid-neuk on going out, and 'carried her home. Next morning she was intro- 'duced to a covered drain, which ran across the 'road, the said drain being closed up at one end, 'whereby she was compelled to give battle to her 'foes. A young terrier was the first to oppose her, 'and paid for its rashness by retreating from the 'drain with the skin almost torn from its nose. 'Another of the same age met with the same punish- 'ment, and Davidson, considerably irritated, brought 'forward Tar, the old dame, who, by her age and 'experience, he considered, would be more than a 'match for the cat. There was sore fighting for a 'time, till again Puss was victorious, and Tar with- 'drew from the conflict in such a condition that her 'master exclaimed, "Confoond the cat, she's tumlit '"an e'e oot o' the bitch!" which indeed was the case. '"Tak awa the stanes frae the tap o' the cundy," 'said Davidson, "and we'll ha'e her worried at '"ance." The stones were removed, and out leapt the 'cat in the middle of her enemies. Fortunately for 'her, however, it happened that a stone wall was con- 'tinued up the side of the road, which she instantly 'mounted, and, running along the top thereof, with 'the dogs in full cry after her, she speedily reached a 'plantation, and eluded all pursuit. No trace of her 'could be discovered; and the next time the shep- 'herd called at Andrew Telfer's house, *my lady* was 'seated on the dresser, as demure as if nothing in 'her whole life had ever disturbed her tranquillity.'

When on the subject of the pluck of the Pepper and Mustard race, I might relate endless stories of the dogs of the olden time. Perhaps one or two of these may, however, not be amiss.

Mr. Somner's famous dog 'Shem' was a son of 'Charlie' (referred to at p. 46), bred by old John Stoddart of Selkirk, and belonging to Thomas Tod, Esq. of Drygrange, and inherited all his father's and grandfather's fighting qualities. The stories of 'Shem's' pluck are endless, but the following may suffice to show what he could do.

One day Mr. Somner happened to be in Kelso on market-day, accompanied by 'Shem.' While in the 'Cross Keys' with a friend, there came down the street an Italian-looking fellow with a large brown dancing-bear,—muzzled, of course, and accompanied by the inevitable 'long pole.' Mr. Somner's friend laughingly said, on seeing the bear, 'Now, Somner, there's something that will frighten '"Shem."' Shem, it may be stated, only weighed

14 lb., while the bear was,—well—considerably more, to say the least of it. Mr. Somner, however, at once replied, 'I'll bet you a five-pound note he will face 'the bear.' 'Done,' says the friend. The only condition made was that the bear was to remain muzzled, and that, if he hugged 'Shem,' he was to be beaten off. After an interview with the landlord, it was arranged that the bear was to be got quietly into the back-yard. The Italian, however, at first demurred to the proposal, but at length said he would like to see the dog before he agreed. When 'Shem' was produced, great was his surprise, for his mind had been running on huge mastiffs and the like. He then laughingly agreed at once. Into the yard they all went. Being market-day, the yard was crowded with gigs and carriages of all descriptions, and, the people getting wind of the affair, these were soon crowded with folk anxious to see the fun.

Mr. Somner took 'Shem' up in his arms, and walking up close to the bear, showed him to 'Shem,' coaxingly asking him if he would like to taste the big brute. 'Shem's' ears cocked, and his eyes gleamed fire by way of answer, and the moment he was loosed he rushed at the bear, and fastened on his snout, sticking there in the most determined way. The bear was as much surprised as the spectators, and loudly roared for mercy. Mr. Somner's friend was asked if he was satisfied, and replying in the affirmative, 'Shem' was taken off the bear, whose attention was first distracted by a liberal use of the long pole.

The bet was divided between the owner of the bear and the Cross Keys' stable lads.

'Shem's' maternal grandfather (belonging to the Marquis of Tweeddale) and great-grandfather came to a somewhat unusual end. A fox had gone to ground, in an earth which had three entrances. As Dr. John Brown describes the scene,[1] 'The father 'was put in at one hole, the son at another, and 'speedily the fox bolted out at the third, but no ap-'pearance of the little terriers, and, on digging, they 'were found dead, locked in each other's jaws; they 'had met, and it being dark, and there being no time 'for explanations, they had throttled each other!'

So much for the gameness of the Dandies of forty years ago. As for the Dandies of the present day, have they the same pluck as their ancestors? I confidently assert they have. In these times, unfortunately, owing to the destruction of vermin all over the country by gamekeepers skilled in the art of trapping, there are not the opportunities for using terriers which there were half a century ago, when game was not nearly so generally or system-

[1] See *Horæ Subsecivæ*, quoted *ante*.

atically preserved in Scotland. Shootings were not then in such request as they are in at the present time, and the result was that, in the more remote districts, the fox, badger, otter, polecat, etc., were able to exist comparatively unmolested, at least when contrasted with the close trapping carried on everywhere nowadays, with the one exception in favour of foxes in hunting districts.

When opportunity offers, however, it will be found that the existing descendants of the Pepper and Mustard race can still creditably sustain the historic family character for pluck.

A well-known breeder and lover of Dandies has supplied the following instance which occurred in 1872. A friend of his, A., who resided in Galloway, desired to get a well-bred Dandie Dinmont puppy, with the view of training it as a vermin terrier. Accordingly in November 1870 a nice dog pup named 'Tartar' (son of a celebrated champion, now dead, and brother of a Dandie who has distinguished himself as the sire and grandsire of many prize-winners) was sent to him. When about a year old 'Tartar' had become 'a fell chiel at the vermin,' as his owner expressed it, having, among other exploits, accounted satisfactorily for a half-grown fox. The following spring (1871) another pup, 'Crab,' was sent to A. to be brought up in the footsteps of

'Tartar,' but it was not until about a year afterwards that an opportunity of testing his courage at 'big game' occurred. 'Crab' would then be about sixteen months old, while 'Tartar' was about two years old.

One evening A. was returning homewards with his son G., having been rabbiting, accompanied by a retriever bitch, 'Judy.' When crossing a small stream near home their attention was attracted by 'Judy' making a dead set at some roots overhanging the stream (a tributary of the Ken, and not very far from that river). From the excited appearance of the bitch there was evidently something more unusual than a rabbit or rat among the roots, and accordingly A. made his son run off to the kennels, which luckily were not far distant, to fetch the terriers 'Tartar' and 'Crab.' By the time this was arranged 'Judy' was much excited, and was madly barking at the foot of the bank. The terriers soon arrived, and 'Tartar,' *seniores priores*, was sent to ground. Almost immediately he was heard in conflict with something, and then all again was still, the 'varmint' having evidently shifted his position beyond the terrier's reach. 'Tartar' shortly appeared, the state of his head giving unmistakeable evidence that he had been in close contact with some hard-bitten foe. 'Crab,' being smaller, was then sent in, and was soon heard to be vigorously engaged with the enemy. 'Tartar' was despatched to his assistance, when a great 'collieshangie' took place, during which 'Judy,' not being able to take part in it, went nearly mad on the bank with excitement. Suddenly the warfare ceased, when G. immediately thereafter observed (and took an ineffective snap-shot at) a large otter slipping silently over the broken water into the pool below. The 'fish-slicer' had bolted under water from his holt unobserved. In the hurry-scurry which ensued G. kept his head, and running at once to the foot of the pool, prevented the otter slipping down stream into a deep glen below. 'Judy' had dashed into the pool, followed by the terriers, but the otter seemed to have vanished. The sagacious 'Judy,' however, was not long in discovering that he had, under cover of the broken bank and rough ground, stolen out of the water, and was attempting the 'overland route' for the neighbouring glen. She at once took up the scent in company with the terriers. The quarry was soon viewed, and the retriever, having the heels of the party, was first in the run up, cleverly catching up her game by the back and turning it over. The terriers, which were close up, ran in and collared the otter before it could recover itself. A great worry then took place, when, after fully testing the courage of the terriers, A. rendered some assistance, and the otter (a large dog weighing 20 lbs.) at last gave up the ghost, not however without having left his mark on the terriers, which had come in for some very severe punishment, 'Crab' in particular being bitten all over head, neck, and chest.

Among several instances of the sterling qualities of the Dandie as a vermin terrier which have of recent years appeared in the sporting journals, I may quote here one which appeared in a letter addressed to the *Live Stock Journal* of 28th April 1882, observing, that having been present on the occasion referred to, I can personally vouch for the accuracy of the narrative :—

To the Editor of the Live Stock Journal.

SIR,—The following note of an encounter with a Scotch hill fox may prove interesting to those of your readers who have 'a 'weakness' for the Dandie Dinmont Terrier, the more so as of late various innuendoes have been made as to the gameness of that terrier.

A friend of mine, whom I will call A., recently asked me to visit him, and have a walk over the hills in his neighbourhood, and, knowing that I kept Dandies, kindly added that he would be happy to see one or two of my favourites with me, as he thought he could guarantee some sport for them in the cairns on his hills. Anxious to have a good stretch over the heather myself, and doubly so as my tykes were also invited, I accepted for myself, and for Badger and Ginger.

Saturday morning saw A., his brother B., and myself, accompanied by Badger and Ginger, start on our walk. We first visited some old fox-earths in one or two sand hillocks, covered with 'scrubby' wood, which stood in the middle of a dreary peat-moss, but after the terriers had explored these in a somewhat lukewarm way, and without finding Reynard at home, we made a move for the higher ground.

I should, perhaps, have mentioned before that Badger and Ginger are respectively dog and bitch, three-year-old Dandies, and that Ginger (in the hands of her former owner) has taken a first at the premier English Show, and was in your valuable *Journal*, if I mistake not, described as 'a beautiful-shaped terrier, 'but too much of a toy.' The 'toy' weighs 17 lbs.! Neither terrier had hitherto seen bigger 'game' than 'rottens' (rats), and these only occasionally.

While we were tramping over the 'moss,' as before mentioned, trying the likely places for a fox, and in making our way up the neighbouring hill to a cairn (some two miles off) we had some heavy snow and hail showers, which rather damped our ardour, not to speak of soaking the terriers, and making their progress through the rough heather and over broken ground rather hard work.

Behold us, however, arrived at a huge conglomeration of boulders, covering a circle of about a hundred yards in circumference. A. pointed out a fissure where he had once seen a fox bolted from, and I accordingly lowered Ginger by the tail into a very ugly-looking place. In a short time, however, I had to fish her up again, as she refused to go any distance into the cairn, but stood shivering with the cold and wet on a ledge of rock, her coat steaming like a 'bus horse on a frosty morning. 'Try her in 'here,' says A.; 'I think she could get along better here.' So in she was thrust again at a different place. This time, however, her behaviour was different. No sooner was she in than she disappeared. A minute or two of silence, then from the depths came first a sharp barking, next a yell of mingled rage and pain, and then sounds of 'high words' between her and some 'unknown beast.' Shortly afterwards the bitch scrambled suddenly out of the cairn at a different place from where she had been put in, having her face cut open, and looking altogether rather dishevelled. In she went again, however, and we heard the fight again begin in a different quarter. Suddenly a fox showed for a moment at a crevice in the rocks, but went in again on seeing B., who was standing near, and we heard the bitch at him next moment. Owing to the large size of the cairn I now thought it might be as well to put Badger in too, it being besides quite likely that there might be more than one fox among the stones. So Badger was put in on the opposite side of the cairn from Ginger. In a minute or two we heard him give tongue beside Ginger, and the sounds proved that they were both into the same fox. After ascertaining the whereabouts of the combatants as nearly as possible, we set about removing the boulders to get down to where they were. The first that was seen of them were the two tails of the terriers sticking out together through between two huge slabs of stone.

Closer inspection showed that whatever they had hold of was beneath one of the 'slabs,' and accordingly we went to work to open up the rear of the stone. This having been done, I put in my arm, and soon got our red friend by the brush. I found, however, that the hole was too small to pull the dogs through, and also that the dogs themselves had got 'jammed' between the rocks. At last, however, we got them clear, when a gory spectacle was seen. Ginger had the fox by the throat, while Badger was securely locked to the fox; the latter having seized him by the muzzle, driving in his canines to their hilts, while Badger had the fox by the lower jaw, and had bitten so hard that he had broken one of the fox's lower canines, and smashed the jaw. It is perhaps unnecessary to say that the fox was just about 'awa' wi 't' by the time we got down to him, and his mask was *not* worth stuffing. Both terriers were pretty severely punished.

The whole performance of the terriers, however, greatly

pleased me, both showing any amount of gameness, which was, perhaps, hardly to be expected, considering, as I have said, neither of them had ever seen before any vermin bigger than a rat. A dram all round to the memory of the late Mr. Fox, and we marched down the hill homewards, well pleased with the afternoon's fun. OLD CRUSTY.

The foregoing anecdotes are, I think, sufficient to show that the Dandie still possesses the pluck which made his ancestors' fame, and that he is, if properly entered, a first-class vermin dog.

As a friend and companion he is equally good. His sagacity, quiet, self-composed, and dignified manners and quaint appearance, all fit him to be a companion; while his fidelity to his master is unsurpassed by any other breed of dog.

The Dandie is an excellent house-dog, being very watchful, and his dignified demeanour when investigating after the manner of dogs (viz., the solemn 'walk round' the object of inquiry with 'birse' erect, and stiffened legs and tail) the social status and respectability of a stranger, is a sight only to be seen to be appreciated. The tramp or beggar-man, on such occasions, puts on his best 'company' manners, for there is that in the little dog's expressive eye and manner which warns him not to take liberties.

Altogether the Dandie is a self-contained little dog, and, while devotedly attached to his master (he prefers to own but one), he quietly goes about his business without fawning for caresses. Like all other old and valued servants, he is thought indeed occasionally, by some, to be a little masterful; but inquiry will usually show that on such occasions he has been unwarrantably interfered with by some one who is *not* his master, and the Dandie, being an intelligent doggie, full well understands the distinction. 'Mind your own business, and I'll attend 'to mine,' is the Dandie's motto.

APPENDIX.

I.—PEDIGREE of Dandie Dinmont Terrier Dog 'SHEM,' bred by MR. F. SOMNER, West Morriston, in 1839, afterwards (1845) the property of E. BRADSHAW SMITH, Esq. of Blackwoodhouse, Ecclefechan. Compiled from Mr. Somner's notes.

'SHEM' was of a bluish black-grey colour, with white head; body long, and arched at loins; short legs; weight, 14 lbs. A dog of great courage, and thoroughly tried at all sorts of 'vermin.' Whelped 1839.

Sire, 'CHARLIE' (No. 1), the property of Thomas Tod, Esq. of Drygrange, by old John Stoddart, Selkirk's, 'Dandie 1.' out of his 'Shan' from Hindlee.

Dam, 'MUSTARD' (Mr. Somner's), by 'Dandie' (No. 2).

G. Dam, by one of the Marquis of Tweeddale's terriers (No. 3).

G.G. Dam, by 'Old Pepper' (No. 4), (Somner's, bred by Allan).

G.G.G. Dam, by 'Davie' (No. 5), (bred by Somner, afterwards belonging to the Earl of Lauderdale).

G.G.G.G. Dam, by 'Salt' (No. 6), (Somner's, and bred by Mr. T. Stevenson, Jedburgh).

G.G.G.G.G. Dam, by 'Wogy Cobawn' (No. 7), (Somner's).

G.G.G.G.G.G. Dam, by 'Fox' (No. 8), (Somner's, bred by Mr. T. Stevenson, Jedburgh), out of 'Nettle' (No. 9), Somner's, and bred by James Davidson, Hindlee (*alias* 'Dandie Dinmont of Charlieshope').

Note 1.—'CHARLIE' was bred by old John Stoddart, the blacksmith at Selkirk, who was generally admitted to have the purest strain of the Dandie Dinmont breed in the Borders. Although his weight was only 12 lb., 'Charlie' had great courage, and would face anything. An example of his pluck is mentioned in the text. 'Charlie's' sire, Stoddart's 'Old Dandie,' was a very handsome, light grey and tan dog, with short legs, and being very broad behind. He was reputed the gamest dog of his day.

'OLD SHAN,' the dam of 'Charlie,' was a small dark grey bitch from Hindlee, with under-shot jaw. She also was very game.

2. 'DANDIE' (Lord Polwarth's) was from the kennel of Sir Walter Scott of Abbotsford, who presented a beautiful dog and bitch to the late Lord Polwarth of Mertoun, as specimens of the pure breed of Dandie Dinmont.

3. The Marquis of Tweeddale's terriers were selected by his Lordship himself from the kennels of the best breeders in the Borders of Scotland, at long prices. The dog which was used in this pedigree was one of the terriers (the son) referred to in the anecdote given at page 123 of the text.

4. 'OLD PEPPER' was purchased by Mr. Somner from a tinker in Yetholm famous for the purity of his breed of Dandie Dinmonts. He was a grandson of old Allan the basketmaker in Hollystone, on the Coquet Water, and declared 'Pepper' to be a true lineal descendant of the famous dog 'Hitchem,' which belonged to his grandfather.

5. 'DAVIE' was a mustard-coloured dog bred by Mr. Somner. He was sold to the Earl of Lauderdale. His weight was 13 lb. only; notwithstanding, he was game enough to stand punishment from the fangs of any vermin that was taken in the traps, from a cat upwards. The gamekeepers declared that 'fear was not in his composition.' 'Davie' was a beautiful specimen of the breed.

6. 'SALT' was a mustard-coloured dog bred by Thomas Stevenson, Esq., Jedburgh, who had a splendid kennel of Dandie Dinmont terriers. He was a first-rate judge of the breed, and an intimate acquaintance of Mr. James Davidson, Hindlee, *alias* 'Dandie Dinmont of Charlieshope,' who was one of his leading men when a day was fixed for a fox-hunt amongst the Cheviot Hills. 'Salt' was about 16 lb. weight, and would encounter anything with a hair on 't. He was sold to a noble-

man at a long price, to go abroad as a perfect specimen of the breed.

7. 'WOGY COBAWN' was bought for Mr. Somner by Mr. Stevenson above mentioned out of a kennel of high repute near Jedburgh. He was of a bluish black colour, intermixed with white hairs, with a head-covering of white hair. Head large; ears pendulous and leathery, covered with the sort of hair recommended in the Dandie Dinmont Club's Standard. He was very handsome, and attracted the attention of all who saw him. This dog was larger in size than the usual run of Mr. Somner's dogs.

8. 'FOX' was presented to Mr. Somner by Mr. T. Stevenson before mentioned, as a stud dog. He had been long in Mr. Stevenson's service, bolting foxes from their strongholds in the Cheviot Hills, and when given to Mr. Somner his teeth were worn to stumps. Yet show him vermin and he was all alive for mischief. 'Fox' was a fine specimen of the breed, having a long flexible body upon short legs.

9. 'NETTLE' was from the kennels of 'Dandie Dinmont' direct. Her colour was a pepper, with white head, dark hazel eye, pendent ears, very long body upon short legs; weight 11 lb. She was very game.

II.—PEDIGREE of 'PODGY II.,' a Pepper Dandie Dinmont Bitch, bred by Mr. E. B. Smith of Blackwoodhouse. Whelped 1853. Died 1864.

- 'PODGY II.' (E. B. Smith's). (*See Illustration.*)
  - 'Podgy I.' (E. B. Smith's).
    - 'Pepper.'—Full sister to 'May-day' (see Illustration, p. 106). By 'Musty;' her dam by 'Tanner;' her g. dam by 'Dusty;' g.g. dam by 'Tuggem;' g.g.g. dam by 'Old Musty.' 'All of which were considered the pure breed.'—D. M'DOUGAL, Cessford, 23d June 1843. (Frain of Trows.)
    - 'Shem.' (F. Somner's.) For Pedigree see Appendix I.
  - 'Dandie (L.)' (E. B. Smith's).
    - 'Ruth' (E. B. Smith's). Bred by Hugh Purves, Leaderfoot.
      - 'Whin.'—Full sister to 'Mustard,' dam of Somner's 'Shem.' (Hugh Purves, Leaderfoot.) For Pedigree see Appendix I.
      - 'Dandie II.'—Full brother to 'Drygrange Charlie.' (J. Stoddart's.) For Pedigree see Appendix I.
    - 'Old Ginger' (E. B. Smith's). Bred at The Haining, Selkirkshire.
      - 'Vixen.' (5th Duke of Buccleuch's).
        - 'Wasp.'—Full sister to 'Drygrange Charlie.' (Mrs. Douglas, Old Melrose.) For Pedigree see Appendix I.
        - 'The Mertoun Dandie.' (Lord Polwarth's.) See Appendix I.
      - 'Old Pepper' (5th Duke of Buccleuch's).

NOTE.—This Pedigree was taken from the Blackwoodhouse Records.

III.—PEDIGREE of Pepper Dandie Dinmont Dog 'DIRK' (The Incomparable).

Bred by Mr. E. B. Smith. Whelped 1865. Died 1877.

- 'DIRK' (The Incomparable) (Mr. E. B. Smith's).
  - Dam, 'Jenny' (Mr. E. B. Smith's).
    - 'Spice II.' (E. B. Smith's).
      - 'Old Tuggem' (E. B. Smith's).
        - 'Spice I.'—Full sister to 'Ruth' (Hugh Purves'). For Pedigree see Appendix II. (E. B. Smith's).
        - 'Dirk I.' (E. B. Smith's).
          - 'Pepper' (Frain's). For Pedigree see Appendix II.
          - 'Dandie II.'—Brother to 'Drygrange Charlie.' (J. Stoddart's.) For Pedigree see Appendix I.
      - Dandie (L.) (E. B. Smith's). For Pedigree see Appendix II.
    - 'Jock.'—Full brother to 'Dandie (B.),' whose Pedigree see below. (E. B. Smith's.)
  - Sire, 'Pepper' (Mr. E. B. Smith's).
    - 'Fanny' (E. B. Smith's).
      - 'Tot' (E. B. Smith's).
        - 'Venom (B.)' (E.B.Smith's).
          - 'Wasp' (Duke of Buccleuch's).
            - 'Shan' (Duke of Buccleuch's). Full sister to 'Drygrange Charlie.' See App. I.
            - 'Pepper' (Duke of Buccleuch's).
          - 'John Pym' (Dr. Brown, Melrose). See Pedigree below.
        - 'Dandie (L.)' (E. B. Smith's). For Pedigree, see Appendix II.
      - 'Ginger' (E. B. Smith's).
        - 'Old Tuggem' (E. B. Smith's).
          - Spice I.—Full sister to 'Ruth,' for whose Pedigree see Appendix II. (E. B. Smith's.)
          - 'Dirk I.' (E. B. Smith's).
            - 'Pepper' (Frain of Trows.) For Pedigree see Appendix II.
            - 'Dandie II.' For Pedigree see App. II. (J. Stoddart's.)
        - Dandie (L.) (E. B. Smith's). For Pedigree see Appendix II.
    - 'Dandie (B.)' (E. B. Smith's).
      - 'Jenny' (Nicol Milne of Faldonside).
        - Pepper bitch. } Both belonging to Ned Dunn, Whitelea, a hunting companion of James Davidson, Hindlee.
        - Yellow dog. }
      - 'John Pym' (Dr. Brown, Melrose).
        - Bitch (John Lauder, Bemerside).
          - 'Pepper' (Frain of Trows). For Pedigree see App. II.
          - 'The Teviotfoot Dandie.'
        - 'Shem' (F. Somner's). For Pedigree see Appendix I.

NOTE.—This Pedigree was taken from the Blackwoodhouse Records.

IV.—PEDIGREE of Pepper Dandie Dinmont Dog 'TWEEDM
the late Mr. J. Robertson, Belzies, near I

- 'TWEEDMOUTH.' (*See Illustration.*)
  - *Dam*, 'Nell' (J. Robertson, Lochmaben).
    - 'Nettle' (J. B. Richardson's).
      - 'Nettle' (Rev. S. T. Mosse's).
        - 'Schann.'—Full sister to I
        - 'Jock.' See below. (N. Milne's.)
      - 'Pepper' (D. Johnstone's, Hawick).
        - 'Tuggem.'—Full sister to ' (E. B. Smith's.)
        - 'Dirk' ('The Incompara (E. B. Smith's).
    - 'Brock' (E. B. Smith's).
      - 'Meg' (Rev. J. C. Macdona).
        - 'Meg' (N. Milne's, Faldonside).
        - 'Jock' (N. Milne's, Faldonside).
          - (
          - (Tur
      - 'Dirk' ('The Incomparable'). See Appen (E. B. Smith's.)
  - *Sire*, 'Shem' (J. B. Richardson, Dumfries), Whelped 1870.
    - 'Tuggem' (J. B. Richardson's).
      - 'Myrtle' (J. B. Richardson's).
        - 'Polly' (T. Russell, Dumfries).
          - 'Alma' (T. Russel
          - 'Pepper (D. Shaw
        - 'Jock' (Wm. Carlyle, Edinburgh
      - 'Pepper.' See Appendix III. (E. B. Smith's.)
    - 'Shamrock' (Rev. S. T. Mosse's), Whelped 1866.
      - 'Vic' (W. Broadwith, Longnewton)
        - 'Maud' (Wm. Johnstone, Lilliesleaf).
          - 'V (J.
          - ' (Miss
        - Dog of good blood belon
      - 'Mustard' (Hodge's), Whelped 1852.
        - 'Nettle' (Boyd's).
          - 'Vi (J. S
          - 'Pep (Sir H. S.
        - 'Pepper' (James Scott, Newstead).
          - 'Jez (J. Sc
          - 'Bra (J. Sc

NOTE.—This Pedigree has been carefully verified from the Blackwoodhouse Records, and other documentary evidence produced.

… Rev. S. T. Mosse's 'Shamrock,' mentioned below.

… the Incomparable 'Dirk.' Appendix III.

…). See Appendix III.

'Old Meg' (… Milne's).

'Badger' (… ll, Hawick).
Turnbull's bitch from Kyle of Braidlea.
'Dandie' (Frain of Trows).

See Appendix III.

'Snugg' (T. Russell's).
'Nettle.'—From Wm. Carlyle, Edinburgh. (T. Russell's).
'Dandie' (Mr. Lyon, Kirkmichael).
'Shan' (J. Stoddart's). 'Dandie I.' (J. Stoddart's). See Appendix I.
'Jerry.'—Bred by Marquis of Abercorn. (Mr. Marsland, Glenae).
'Pepper.'—Bred by E. B. Smith, and same blood as his 'Pepper.'

'Wasp.' See below. (J. Scott's.)

'Little Spice' (J. Scott's).
'Spice' (Johnstone's).
'Nettle' (Brisbane's).
'Pepper' (Sir George Douglas).
'Brandy.' See below. (Jas. Scott's.)

(… Mather's).

Wood's Dog (Ellengrove, Cumberland).
'Viper' (E. B. Smith).
'Wasp' (E. B. Smith).
'Tib' (Pringle of The Haining).
'Dandie' (Pringle of The Haining).
Sister and Brother.
'Wasp' (Mrs. Douglas), Sister to Drygrange 'Charlie.' App. I.
'Dandie' (Lord Polwarth's). See Appendix I.
'Hitchem' (E. B. Smith). By 'Sham,' Appendix I., out of 'May-day,' Appendix II.
'Dirk I.' See Appendix III. (E. B. Smith).

… to an Officer at Piershill Barracks.

'Spice.'—Bred by M'Dougall, Cessford. (Brisbane's.)
'Pepper' (Brisbane's).
'Nettle.'—Bred by Mr. Lyon of Kirkmichael. (Brisbane's).
'Demon' (Brisbane's).
'Pepper' (John Reid's), who at an early period had his Terriers from James Davidson.
'Friar Tuck.' (Frain of Trows. Bred by Mr. Oliphant, Marifield.)

'Schann' (Sir George Douglas).
'Schann.'—Sister to Drygrange 'Charlie.' See Appendix I. (Duke of Buccleuch's).
'Pepper' (Duke of Buccleuch's).
'Pepper I.' Bred by Mr. Lang. (Sir George Douglas.)

'Bess' (J. Scott's).
'Mustard.' See below. (J. Scott's.)
'Old Pepper.'—*Sire*, 'The Slater' (Wat. Leithead), accidentally shot in 1833. Colour grey and tan. (Sir G. Douglas.) Died very old, about 1842. Bred by Mr. Taylor, Whitelee.

'Wasp' (J. Scott's).
'Vic' (J. Scott's).
'Pepper' (J. Scott's).

'Wasp' (J. Scott's).
'Nettle' (J. Scott's).
'Ringlet.'—A grand-daughter of (J. Scott's). Lord Polwarth's 'Dandie.'
'Miss Whisker' (J. Scott's).
'Wasp' (J. Scott's).
'Wasp' (Mr. Sitwell, Barmour).
'The Slater' (Wat. Leithead).
'Dandie' (Lord Polwarth's). See Appendix I.
'Dandie' (Rev. T. Thomson, Maxton Manse).
'Dandie' (Duke of Buccleuch's).
'Dandie' (J. Scott's).
'Mustard.'—Descended from 'The Slater' and Lord Polwarth's 'Dandie.' (J. Scott's).
Drygrange 'Charlie.' See Appendix I.

'Puck.'—Bred by Henry Dodd.—*Sire*, 'Pepper;' *Dam*, 'May-day.'
Dr. Brown.

V.—PEDIGREE of Pepper Dandie Dinmont Terrier Bitch 'BORDER QUEEN.' The property of Mr. W. E. Easten, Hull. Bred by Mr. William Foster, Carlisle. Whelped 11th June 1877. Weight, 19 lbs.

'BORDER QUEEN.' (*See Illustration.*)	*Dam*, 'Ruby' (Mr. Foster's, Carlisle).	'Nettle.' See Appendix IV. (Mr. J. B. Richardson's.)	
		'Shem.' See Appendix IV. (Mr. J. B. Richardson's.)	
	Sire, 'Davie' (Mr. Redford, Silloth).	'Tatters' (Mr. E. B. Smith's).	'Brock' (Mr. E. B. Smith's). — 'Fanny.' See Appendix III. (Mr. E. B. Smith's.)
			'Brock' (Mr. E. B. Smith's). — 'Jock.' Brother to 'Dandie (B).' See Appendix IV. (Mr. E. B. Smith's.)
			'Boxer' (Mr. E. B. Smith's). — 'Old Tuggem.' See Appendix III. (Mr. E. B. Smith's.)
			'Boxer' (Mr. E. B. Smith's). — 'Dandie (L.).' See Appendix II. (Mr. E. B. Smith's.)
		'Dirk' (The Incomparable). See Appendix III. (Mr. E. B. Smith's.)	

NOTE.—This Pedigree has been verified from the Blackwoodhouse Records, and other documentary evidence produced.

MAP SHOWING THE

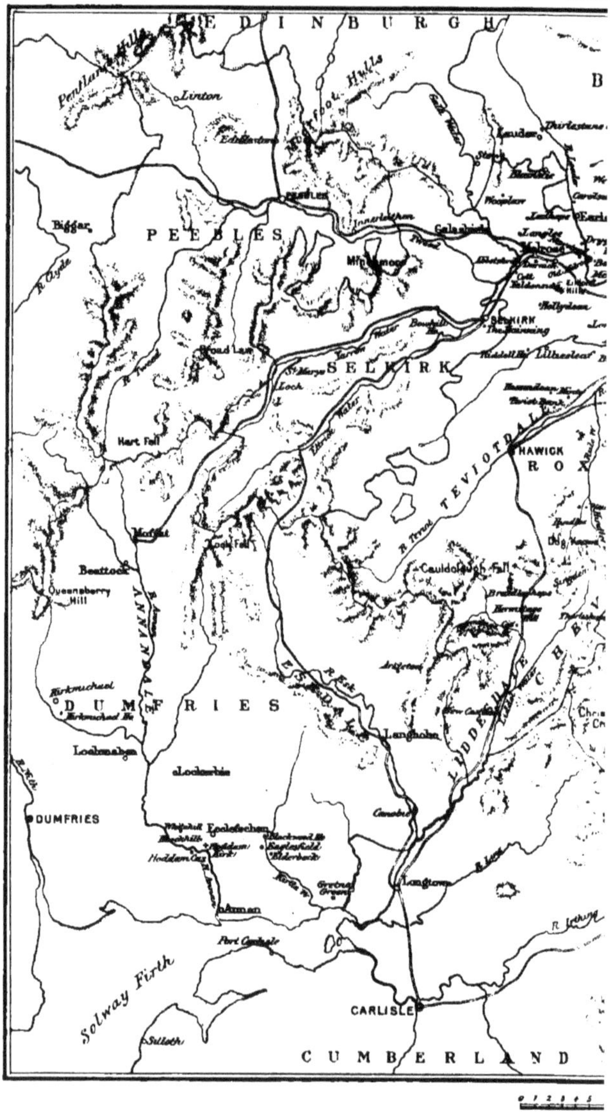

THE DANDIE DINMONT COUNTRY

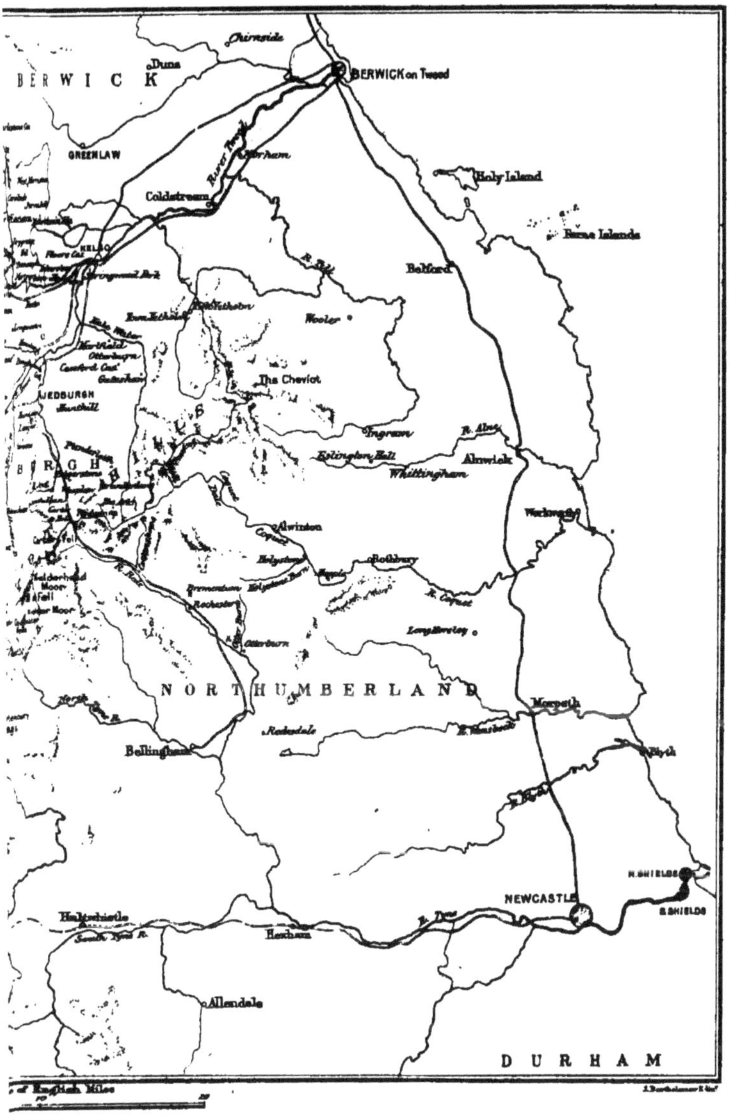

www.ingramcontent.com/pod-product-compliance
Ingram Content Group UK Ltd.
Pitfield, Milton Keynes, MK11 3LW, UK
UKHW020622271125
9218UKWH00003B/92

9 781015 491465